I0062068

PATH PAVER

Copyright © 2024 by Cody Alimondi

All rights reserved.

No portion of this book may be reproduced in any form without written permission from the publisher or author, except as permitted by U.S. copyright law.

This publication is designed to provide accurate and authoritative information in regard to the subject matter covered. It is sold with the understanding that neither the author nor the publisher is engaged in rendering legal, investment, accounting or other professional services. While the publisher and author have used their best efforts in preparing this book, they make no representations or warranties with respect to the accuracy or completeness of the contents of this book and specifically disclaim any implied warranties of merchantability or fitness for a particular purpose. No warranty may be created or extended by sales representatives or written sales materials. The advice and strategies contained herein may not be suitable for your situation. You should consult with a professional when appropriate. Neither the publisher nor the author shall be liable for any loss of profit or any other commercial damages, including but not limited to special, incidental, consequential, personal, or other damages.

Book Cover by Stefano Buro

First edition 2024

ISBN 979-8-9912097-0-0

✸ Created with Vellum

For the mavericks who embrace the adventure of life with courage and authenticity.

PREFACE

*Do not go where the path may lead, go instead where there is
no path and leave a trail.*

— RALPH WALDO EMERSON

Work outlines our identity: who we are as individuals, as
people, as professionals. The relationship we cultivate with
our work and the way in which we understand its relationship to who we are, who we can become, and the life we
experience is pivotal. We often underestimate the importance of work in our lives.

Our modern-day relationship with work stems from a
misunderstanding and therefore a misplacement of its
importance. Today, work is looked at as a necessary evil,
something to do less of. The Faustian bargain—a deal with
the devil in which you trade moral values for a material
thing—has turned into a Faustian riddle: a game with the
devil in which you try to outsmart him.

The modern Faustian bargain involves the exchange of
time for money: in other words, long work hours for large

compensation. The modern Faustian riddle involves finding a way to gain money with minimal work hours: in other words, working less but retaining large compensation. In both scenarios, work is viewed as something to deal with, a problem to solve and eliminate. Modern work, for most of us, is simply about financial acquisition.

We have not always had this style of relationship with work. Our professional work is influential to how we experience life, to who we become and our discovery of who we are. Given that, we should choose our work with courage and purpose, but this is far from an easy task or ask.

The goal of *Path Paver* is to serve as a metaphorical framework to leverage in pursuit of interesting work, a kind of work that provides meaning, purpose, and fulfillment. We need an alternative way to think about work, and this book seeks to provide that alternative. The only way to forever escape the pull of Faustian arrangements is to cultivate a relationship with your work. In other words, your professional work should mean something to you, so you cannot simply be bought, just as no amount of money could ever convince me to sell my kids. Your professional work becomes a part of you because it is a part of you. There is no paved path you can follow to interesting professional work; you must pave your own.

If you stop reading here, take one thing away: The professional work you choose to do matters. It matters in who you are, who you become, and the life you experience.

Before we explore this new way of thinking about work, it's important that I define a few key terms that I will refer to throughout the book:

Professional work: This is work that we do at a level at which we compete with other professionals. Our professional work should interest us, but unfortunately that is rarely the case.

Interesting work: This can be defined as work we do that brings us excitement, purpose, meaning, and fulfillment. Unfortunately, the majority of modern work is far from interesting. Part of that is by design, and part of that results from the modern attitude we have toward work. More on this later.

Path paver: This is an individual who chooses to pave their own path in pursuit of interesting work. They forgo the well-paved professional paths for the dangerous adventure of a lifetime.

The pursuit of interesting work is noble, but why does it really matter? For some, it won't. However, there are others who desire to spend energy on something that provides them meaning, purpose, and fulfillment, and to do it at a professional level. If we spend a lifetime in professional work that we find interesting instead of professional work we find tolerable, the difference in our life experience will be great.

One thing to note: Professional work isn't simply about money. We won't talk about money at all in this book. Money actually isn't a requirement for something to be considered professional work. (Olympians and grandparents are not paid, after all.) Nevertheless, if you are performing at a professional level, especially today, there are many creative ways to earn revenue.

By the end of this short book, my hope is that you will accept the call to adventure and find the courage to pave your own path to interesting work.

CONTENTS

WORK
DIFFERENT & FAMILIAR

The price of anything is the amount of life you exchange for it.

— HENRY DAVID THOREAU

The opportunity to experience life is unique to every one of us, yet often we strive to outsource our individuality in pursuit of something that is not authentic. We look to experts, celebrities, or wealthy individuals to show us the way, to provide insight in how we should experience life, what we should do, and the work required to be deemed successful.

But what if we have reached an era when imitation is a sure way to failure? What if following the well-paved path is a sure way to destruction? Maybe it's time for an evolution in our philosophy and how we approach an essential element of who we are: our professional work.

The modern approach to work has the scent of necessary evil to it. The idea of enjoying your work is not essential; if you do, that's fine, but it's not a requirement. Over the last hundred years, professional work has gone through many iterations, yet the underlying tone has remained the same: work hard, earn a paycheck, and maybe, if you are intelligent with your finances, you can retire one day and not engage in professional work at all. Today, the riddle is figuring out how to engage in professional work less and earn more. Professional work is a means to an end, rarely something we enjoy, let alone find meaning, purpose, or fulfillment in.

It has not always been this way, though. For most of *Homo sapiens'* existence, professional work was an integral part of who we were, our identity, and it dictated the way in which we experienced life. Whether it was in hunter-gatherer communities, early civilizations, or massive empires, the professional work individuals did was a representation of who they were. Over time, our relationship with work shifted as a reflection of the design of work. For most of our history, our work was something that connected us to the community, to society, and, most important, to ourselves. It was an essential element of our life. The professional work we engaged in was important work, work that was required for survival. By design, this work provided meaning: we were engaging in professional work that had a direct impact on the prosperity of our community. It provided fulfillment, as it feels good to be of value, and purpose, as we knew our work mattered.

However, our relationship to professional work has become less and less connected due to a change in the design of work. Two elements that have influenced this new design are the development of optionality and opportunity. Optionality relates to the expansion of the number of different types of professional work available, and opportunity relates to reduced barriers for a profession.

For a long time, most people didn't have much say in

the professional work they did; it was a birth lottery system. If you were born into a blacksmith's family, odds were you would become a blacksmith; if you were born a male in Spartan society, you were a warrior. Then there came a change: prosperity provided options and opportunities, and this led to a new work design and a fracture in our relationship with work.

Today we live in an era in which the opportunity for individuals to engage in professional work they find interesting is unprecedented. Please do not mistake interesting for easy. Work will always require a degree of suffering and sacrifice; the difficult task is deciding what we will suffer for, and which sacrifices we will make. The growth of professional work opportunity and optionality naturally presents the paradox of choices, and the challenge of choosing.

THE PARADOX OF CHOICES

The paradox of choices is the idea that there comes a point at which we have too many choices and in the end are never satisfied with our choice because we don't know whether we made the right one.

I once heard a story about a man who went to get some cheese. There were two cheese shops, located across the street from each other. The first one was this beautiful cheese factory where wheels of cheese filled the walls. Rumor was they had over three hundred different types of cheese.

One day a man went into this shop. He was in awe of such a production. The owner greeted him like royalty and gave him the red-carpet treatment, allowing him to try any cheese he desired. The man was in heaven and tried cheese after cheese. Then they all began to taste the same: the man couldn't tell the difference between the cheeses. Now came the time to decide what cheese he was going to purchase, and he felt overwhelmed.

In the end, he picked one but went home questioning his choice. The experience started off exciting but ended up overwhelming and stressful. The man appreciated and enjoyed the cheese factory but was not in a hurry to go back.

The next time the man needed cheese, he decided to go to the other cheese shop, across the street. This shop shared characteristics with the first one, but there was one big difference: it carried only five cheeses, and two of them were seasonal.

This cheese shop owner, just like the previous one, treated the man like royalty and rolled out the red carpet for him. The owner brought the man to a table where he had wine set up and a board of testers of each cheese. The factory owner and the man had a nice conversation, enjoying each cheese slowly.

In the end, the man picked a seasonal wheel of cheese and felt confident and happy with his choice. The experience that had started off exciting ended with bliss. The man brought his cheese home, excited to share it with his family and friends and, more important, to talk about his experience.

Having some options is better than having none, but there comes a point at which having too many options is stressful and overwhelming. If you have clarity regarding your skills, talents, abilities, character, and knowledge, it becomes easier to identify favorable options. You understand your tastes and preferences and the environments in which you can prosper. As the old Seneca saying goes, "If a man knows not to which port he sails, no wind is favorable."

THE CHALLENGE OF CHOOSING

The paradox of choices creates the challenge of choosing. When we have extensive optionality, we struggle to choose because of the fear of making the wrong decision. Often, we make professional work decisions based on societal criteria, not personal criteria. Our choices are driven by the identity that comes with the work; we don't make the choices that would reflect our preferences, dispositions, and interest.

It's far too common for individuals to get too far down a certain path and feel that they cannot turn around and start over. This is often referred to as the sunk-cost fallacy. Another common problem caused by the challenge of choosing is that individuals don't get started because they don't want to commit to something if they are not all in. I refer to these individuals as aimlessly wandering. Either way, with a vast amount of optionality, we get overwhelmed with choices and struggle to make a sound one.

The cost is that we make "safe" choices over authentic or personally appropriate choices. We overlook the opportunities presented by the modern world because we're overwhelmed by choices, and by default, we fail to seize any opportunities. We prefer making a safe mistake to making a dumb mistake, and when it comes to professional work, we choose the well-paved path. Anything off that well-paved path is considered dumb, silly, and reckless. So when it comes to the challenge of choosing professional work in the modern era, we are paralyzed, as the variety of choices overwhelms us. We choose the safe route for our situation and social environment, thinking if we don't succeed, at least we "failed" safely.

DESIGN AND ATTITUDE

The way something is designed will naturally influence our attitude in some way. Consider how a restaurant does lighting and chooses the music, or how a Frank Lloyd Wright house makes you feel as you walk through each room. Designed with intention, it influences our feelings and experience. To have a clear understanding of our relationship to professional work, it's necessary to discuss how professional work design influences our attitude about professional work.

Important professional work is work that is essential to survival. Its design is personal, useful, and communal. It leads an individual to feel they have meaning, purpose, and fulfillment. A hunter who kills a big animal for their community feels purposeful because they engage in professional work to achieve a big game kill. The hunter feels meaning because they are an essential part of the community: without food, the community suffers. The hunter feels fulfillment because they successfully engage in their professional work, that of providing. Altogether, this gives life much meaning and direction; however, it is important to note the hunter most likely did not have a choice to become a hunter. An individual who operates in this type of work design rarely feels psychologically lost.

Structured and safe professional work is work that is chosen for social and financial reasons. Its design is general, efficient, and standardized. The attitude that follows is that of financial responsibility, social status,

pursuing a means to an end, and engaging with work as a necessary evil. A lawyer who logs an eighty-hour week feels purposeful because they accomplished many tasks and earned the firm money. The lawyer feels meaning because they are a respected part of society: without lawyers, innocent people would be penalized. The lawyer feels fulfillment because they successfully engaged in their professional work, providing financial rewards for their family. However, what we commonly find is that the actual professional work suffocates the lawyer as an individual. They don't find purpose, meaning, or fulfillment in the legal tasks they perform. They pursued this profession for reasons that did not reflect who they were as a person, an individual. An individual in this situation commonly feels psychologically lost.

Structured and safe work design creates professional work prisons: you serve your time by making enough money to retire, then avoid professional work for the rest of your life. With this new design, professional work transitions from a part of who we are, an authentic identity, (important work), to a part we can't wait to get rid of and an inauthentic identity (structured and safe work).

Interesting professional work is work that is chosen on the basis of our interests. Its design is personal, joyful, and idiosyncratic. An individual engaged in interesting professional work feels meaning, purpose, fulfillment, and a sense of identity. What we notice is a contrast with important work, where identity is not included; this is simply because most individuals did not have a choice of work due to lack of opportunities and optionality. So, the individual engaged in important work submerges their personal identity in favor of identifying with the collective. In the words of Erich Fromm, "the individual ceases to be himself; he adopts entirely the kind of personality offered to him by cultural patterns; and he therefore becomes exactly as all others are and as they expect him to be... The person who gives up his individual self and becomes an automaton, identical with millions of other automatons around him, need not feel alone and anxious anymore. But the price he pays, however, is high; it is the loss of his self."

In structured and safe professional work, an individual chooses a type of work and then builds an identity around it. In interesting work, an individual cultivates their individuality and chooses work that suits it. We cannot be anything and everything we put our minds to; that's wishful thinking, a path to delusion. If we acknowledge that we are simply not suited for some types of professional work, the paradox of choices and the challenge of choosing begin to loosen their reins. If we fail to do this, we become overwhelmed and blindly make a deal with the devil.

THE FAUSTIAN BARGAIN AND RIDDLE

The term *Faustian bargain* originates from the classic play *Faust*, by Johann Wolfgang von Goethe. To begin with, its protagonist, Faust, is very successful, at least in general terms, but is unhappy with his life. From the outside, Faust's life looks full, but on the inside it's empty. One day Faust is visited by Mephistopheles, the devil, and is offered a bargain: in exchange for his soul, Faust will be rewarded with unlimited knowledge and material pleasure.

For the purposes of this book, the Faustian bargain serves as a metaphor for the way we choose professional work. We sacrifice something valuable for something that is shiny but far less valuable. In other words, we sacrifice who we are, who we could become, and how we experience life for money, power, and social status, none of which can provide us with authentic meaning, purpose, or fulfillment. How many financially successful individuals in this world are unsatisfied with life and who they are or have become? The Faustian bargain is a deal that many have unconsciously agreed to.

The Faustian riddle is my twist on the classic bargain, as today professional work has become a game of passive income. How can we do as little work possible or retire as early as possible but also earn money while achieving power and social status? The Faustian riddle is not far from the Faustian bargain; the difference here is time. In the latter, time is all but expected: if you want to be "successful," you have to work hard. However, now, in the riddle, it's about doing it with less time spent. How can we spend the least amount of time engaging in professional work while being financially secure?

The Faustian bargain and riddle are deals we no longer need to make. When we operate in the work design of structured and safe work, we have limited avenues to take in which we can avoid these deals. Sure, it's possible, but you are swimming upstream. But if we operate by paving our own path in the pursuit of interesting professional work, we naturally develop liberation from such deals. However, this comes at a price, and the cost is a dangerous adventure—the type of adventure only heroes have the courage to accept.

THE ADVENTURE OF INTERESTING WORK

The hero's journey is one that we will refer to frequently, as that is what path pavers are by nature: heroes in the making. Anyone who discovers, cultivates, and then shares their interesting work with the world at a professional level is a hero. We look up to these individuals, admire them, and sometimes even worship them.

We all can be heroes in life, but that doesn't mean it's easy. Every hero's journey is filled with challenges, problems, and barriers—or what I like to refer to as dragons—that must be vanquished. If we have (or are in pursuit of) professional work that interests us, those challenges, problems, and barriers are not a question of if but of how and when.

If we engage in work we don't find interesting, we will simply avoid the challenges, problems, and barriers, and by ignoring them, we bypass the opportunity to ignite elements inside us that lie dormant. As Eleanor Roosevelt once said, "sometimes it is the opportunity that brings out the qualities of the individual." In other words, we don't know what we are made of until we are tested. Over the course of the hero's journey, mistakes give us scars that make us interesting and individual.

Finding interesting work is less a choice than it is an adventure, a quest, a journey, a discovery. When you commit to path paving, a personal adventure begins, and you become a hero in the making.

HERO NONNEGOTIABLE #1: DO THE WORK ONLY YOU CAN DO

In all hero stories, the protagonist's journey, adventure, or quest is a reflection of them. The challenges that must be overcome, the help/aids that assist them on the journey, and the sacrifices that must be made are tailored to them. The skills, talents, abilities, character, and knowledge the protagonist develops and earns on the journey prepare them for each step, each phase, until they reach the final climax and become the hero.

The same idea can be leveraged in our pursuit of interesting work. When we follow a paved path, or outlined career path, sooner or later we will get to a point in the path at which we no longer fit. This could be age. It could be skills, talents, abilities, knowledge, or character. It could be lack of timing, could be a variety of things, but sooner or later the paved path will no longer complement us, and then we will be lost without path-paving capabilities. A debilitating place to be.

However, if we choose to pave our own path toward interesting work, regardless of whether we are on a paved path for a restricted amount of time, we are never lost, because with the ability to pave our path, we can wander with purpose.

Our professional work changes with our seasons of life and the development of our character. The idea that we must choose at an early age the professional work we do for a lifetime is nonsense. It's a reflection of the work design of structured and safe work and the related attitudes we have adopted. Each season of life will influence our interests and the professional choices we make. What is true is that interesting work alters with time, and it is not always obvious that the work we are doing now contributes to our interesting work later.

If we pave our path to interesting work, we will cultivate skills, abilities, talents, knowledge, and our character in a way that is personal, and in doing so we will be able to engage in professional work in a way that only we can (idiosyncratically). If we follow a paved path, then we will cultivate skills, abilities, talents, knowledge, and character in a way that is general, and in doing so we will engage in professional work in a way that anyone who fits the path could do.

To simplify this point, let's take the analogy of purchasing suits. You can buy a suit three different ways. First, you can go to a store and buy it off a rack. You may get lucky, and it may fit you just fine. Second, you can go to a store and buy it off a rack and then have it tailored to you. Third and finally, you can build your own suit by picking the material and working with the tailor for the exact cut you want, and the suit will be crafted for you. The suit will be built to conform to any idiosyncratic features you have.

Let's say three men each buy suits, and each use a different option. While all three men are wearing suits, and maybe all three look good in their suits, only one suit is built for the man. For this last man, the man wears the suit; the suit doesn't wear the man. That is the difference. You may not be able to tell the difference between these men when you look at them, but you can tell when you work with them. Similarly, the man who tailors his work to himself produces a different type of work: the work fits him; he doesn't fit himself to the work.

Doing professional work in a way only you can do is participating in interesting professional work. It's the way out of the game of imitation and the way into the game of authentic creation and expression. The work we do is an expression of who we are, who we can become, and our journey along the way. Our work is important and influences the way we experience life; ideally, at the end of our professional work adventure, we become the most interesting versions of ourselves.

HERO NONNEGOTIABLE #2: TREAT WORK AS AN ADVENTURE

There are individuals in the world who engage in interesting work—though not nearly enough. The one thing all these individuals have in common is that the path to their work was not obvious; it was one they paved.

This is reminiscent of the tale of the Holy Grail, in which King Arthur and his knights had a vision of the Holy Grail, a treasure that would help restore the world. As King Arthur and the knights embarked on their journey to find the Grail, they came upon a forest and decided that each of them should enter at a point that he himself had chosen, where it was darkest and there was no path. If there is a path, it is someone else's path, and you are not on the adventure. Any other way would be the wrong way. Each knight paved their own path into the woods and participated in the adventure.

The story and metaphor represent everything the path paver is about: the pursuit of discovery, individuality, and self-reliance. If we approach professional work with the same mentality, it's only a matter of time before we discover interesting work. Unfortunately, we are taught to enter the forest in the same place, at the same spot, and at the same time—a sure way to never find the Holy Grail or, in our terms, interesting work.

Our professional work should be something that aids us in discovering who we are, helps us awaken dormant talents, and allows us to provide something of value to the society or community around us. In a world full of talent, the opportunity for us to recalibrate our philosophy and attitude toward professional work is unprecedented. And it's one that we should neither take for granted nor let slip by. Our professional work journey is a quest by nature; we just have to find the courage to accept the call to adventure.

So this book is an exploration of another way to approach work—to begin the adventure of finding interesting work. In other words, professional work that is chosen by your interests and that provides purpose, meaning, and fulfillment. Then, and only then, can you become the hero of your life, discover who you are, and live authentically.

PART 1
IMPORTANT WORK

*No man is more unhappy than he who never faces
adversity. For he is not permitted to prove himself.*

— SENECA

1

A STORY ABOUT AN ITALIAN

*You can never cross the ocean unless you have the courage to
lose sight of the shore.*

— CHRISTOPHER COLUMBUS

The year was 1979. A young Italian immigrant
accepted the call to adventure, leaving his home, a
small village in Calabria, part of the southern
region of Italy. At the ripe age of twenty, he set his sails to
go to the one place he heard had professional work opportunity: the United States. Never having ventured out of Italy
before, knowing no English, and having limited education
—on one of the rare days he was at school he received an F
on an assignment, and he thought it simply stood for
Franco, his name—he took a leap of faith, to say the least,
in accepting this call to adventure. When an individual has
limited choices, we see what their character is made of and
the depths of their courage—and they, too, make the same

discovery. In that moment the young immigrant learned more about himself than he had in his previous twenty years.

Upon his arrival in the United States, he began working three different jobs to pay bills and survive. Although he was a resourceful individual, his talents were not obvious to employers. Coupled with his lack of ability to speak English, that meant his professional work options were limited. His first three jobs were as follows: in the mornings, he worked in a factory; in the evenings, he repacked produce at a grocery store; and on the weekends, he made pizza at a restaurant.

The young immigrant's life followed this path for a few years until one day he received a job opportunity to be a produce picker at the Chicago Water Street Market. This was a big opportunity for him because it would provide him with enough money that he would no longer have to work multiple jobs. Yet there was a catch: the opportunity was not a sure thing. The company offered him a thirty-day trial (in modern rhetoric, we call this a one-month contract to hire). Given the context of the situation, Franco didn't feel like he could afford to quit the other jobs—they had been hard for him to get in the first place. So, he decided to drop one of them and work the other two. However, after a few weeks of working three jobs and falling asleep at the wheel, he realized there was no other option but to go all in and commit to the produce picking opportunity. He accepted another call to adventure, believed in himself, and succeeded in securing the job at the Chicago produce market. The faith he had in himself would prove to be the difference maker for the rest of his life.

When we look at the job of a produce picker, we may not think anything of it. It's a low-level job that doesn't pay much better than minimum wage. Franco, however, saw it as a great opportunity. He had been raised on a farm in Southern Italy and loved produce. Plus, at the time, the produce world was full of immigrants: Greeks, Italians, Spaniards, you name it. With no other options, Franco developed the courage to be uncomfortable and earn his way through the filth—*in sterquiliniis invenitur*. In other words, he worked from the bottom up.

Fast-forward three years later, and Franco was now a well-liked produce picker and had developed relationships and rapport with produce buyers on the market. As a naturally social, outgoing, and friendly individual, the Italian had a magnetic personality. He would offer information to buyers on what produce looked good and what to stay away from. Predictably, customers saw the value in this young, motivated immigrant and wanted to work with him —plus, they liked him; in a way, he was one of them. Finally, one day Franco mustered up the courage and approached his boss to ask for an opportunity to become a produce salesman. The boss laughed in his face and said no. How could someone who spoke broken English find success selling produce?

Franco, once again putting faith in himself, respectfully put in his two-week notice, ready to go to another spot on the Water Street Market to ask for the same opportunity. The owner of the company caught wind of the situation and intervened. He said they were giving this young man the opportunity he asked for because he had been their best produce picker, customers loved him, and he was a loyal hard worker. The owner of the company realized he had nothing to lose by giving the young man an opportunity but much to lose by letting him leave. So Franco got his request, but the boss didn't like being overruled by the owner (he had a weak ego). Thus, while the boss agreed to give him an opportunity, he stacked the chips against Franco.

Just like before, Franco was given a trial period to sell produce. The catch was that he could only sell three items, and they could not be items that other produce salespeople were already selling. The Italian, being the savvy individual he was, decided to let his boss pick which three produce items he could sell so when he proved himself, his success would be undeniable. After the trial period he would earn the opportunity to sell additional produce items.

Okra, baby eggplant, and finger hot peppers were the only items Franco was authorized to sell. Most produce salespeople would have been dead in the water with this portfolio; however, he was not most salespeople. A hero in the making, he saw this simply as another challenge and was ready to slay this dragon.

As an immigrant who'd grown up in a small town working all types of odd jobs, including farmwork on the side of the Calabrian mountains, Franco understood produce and hard work. More importantly, during his time as produce picker, he'd developed relationships with different produce buyers and paid close attention to their needs. One of the relationships Franco developed was with a Greek immigrant buyer. The world works in serendipitous ways: lo and behold, the Greek buyer bought at scale Franco's limited portfolio of produce, as it fit his grocery store's shopper demographic perfectly.

While Franco was crushing his trial period, he also helped other salespeople sell their produce when they were in a pinch. Since he couldn't, at the time, sell tomatoes, when another salesperson had too many tomatoes, he would take them off that salesperson's hands and sell them to his own buyers—never receiving the credit or recognition, but that didn't matter to him. He was playing chess while everyone else was playing pin the tail on the donkey.

Franco was committed to becoming a true asset to his clients and gaining respect and rapport among his colleagues. He didn't expect anything to be given to him, so he went out and took the opportunity by the horns. As the Spartan King Leonidas famously said when the Persian messenger told them to put down their weapons, *Molon labe*: "Come and take them."

Over the next two years, Franco developed his produce ecosystem, fostering relationships with farmers, logistics professionals, and other industry professionals. At the ripe age of twenty-seven, this young man became the number one produce salesperson at the Chicago Water Street Market, and he held that position for the next twenty-five years, remaining loyal to the company and to the owner who had given him the opportunity, turning down many job offers that would have doubled or tripled his salary.

Franco and the owner of the company were not the only ones who benefited, as early in his sales career, Franco partnered with a farmer who had four acres of farmland. Together they worked hard and expanded operations each year, buying more acres and diversifying their portfolio of produce. Fast-forward twenty-five years, and four acres turned into four hundred. The list of positive ripple effects Franco had on the produce industry and on those in his life could be a book in itself.

This Italian immigrant is my father. His story inspired me from the moment I began to learn about it, and it inspires me to this day. I've learned so much from his journey and the adventures he had along the way. I have no doubt that my interest in and passion for talent and professional work stems from his story. A young man with nothing became a man with something. Every barrier or obstacle you could think of, he encountered. Everything was earned. He is an undeniable legend in his profession. When it is all said and done, he will have left his mark not only on the produce industry but on his family, elevating them from poverty and providing opportunity for the next generation: a selfless gift. He is no different from the individual who plants a tree today so the next generation can enjoy its shade.

My father is unquestionably my first hero, so it was natural for me to take in interest in his professional work. What I found early on was that my father's work was quite different from that of everyone else's parents around me. For one, he left for work at 12:30 a.m. and returned home at 3:30 p.m., at which point we would eat dinner, and by 6:00 p.m. he was sleeping. His schedule reflected that of the produce world: in the morning my father would sell grocery stores their produce, and then in the afternoon he would buy produce for the following day. I realized that where most other jobs were standard nine-to-fives, the schedule for professional work isn't universal; it's contextual. In other words, it depends on the domain and the profession. I found this interesting, asked more questions, and learned that many other aspects of my father's professional work were different.

After so many years, what I have come to realize is that my father's work was different not simply because of his profession or domain but because of him. He was a path paver: he found professional work that was truly interesting to him, and he loved it. It was part of him; it provided meaning, fulfillment, and purpose.

When my mother passed away, he took time off work to

care for me, but after a certain point he needed to go back to work so we could survive and, I believe, so that he could survive, too—and not in the physical sense. Having interesting work allowed him to gain hope and provided belief that life was still worth living, that this shadow would pass, and that the light would remain. I sometimes wonder what would have happened if my father didn't have interesting work but instead had "safe work." Would he have turned to another vice for meaning, fulfillment, and purpose? Who knows, but what I do know is that when life is hard, challenging, or absurd, if we have interesting work, we can weather the storm much more easily. When we participate in interesting professional work, it provides a sense of direction, purpose, fulfillment, and meaning. I believe professional work has always served that role in our lives, even though in the past we didn't refer to it as "professional work."

2

A BRIEF HISTORY OF WORK

Much of the difference between what is work and what is leisure is branding

— NASSIM TALEB

Work is an important element of how we experience life as human beings, who we become as individuals, and what we are as a society, a collective. When we review history, it is the work that survives that tells the story, that moves us and inspires us. Whether we visit the Trevi Fountain in Rome to make a wish or we propose to our partner under the Eiffel Tower, the work of our ancestors still connects with us today.

When we study the history of work, we can begin to modify our attitude toward work and form greater clarity about why work is the way it is today and how we can rebuild a relationship with it. To understand how work fits into who we are and our lives, we seek to understand what work meant to our ancestors—its origins. The idea of work has gone through iterations over the generations and in our history as *Homo sapiens*. The culture and the heroes of each moment in time leave an imprint on it.

Homo sapiens has an interesting history with work. A definition of work that fits the history of *Homo sapiens'* work activities is simple but rarely considered in this light: in the words of anthropologist James Suzman, work involves "purposefully expending energy or effort on a task to achieve a goal or end."

According to Suzman, data suggest that for 95 percent of our species' history, work did not occupy anything like the hallowed place in people's lives that it does now. For most of our ancestors, work was a part of who they were, and there was a sacred nature to it, one that was also connected to the seasons of life and to their maturation process as individuals. Take, for example, a hunter-gatherer tribe. When boys came of age, it was time for them to go through initiation and become men within the tribe. The initiation process of one tribe was one in which the men of the tribe, wearing masks that little boys feared, would come take them from their mothers, and the boys were forced to fight the men in the masks. The men in the masks, fellow tribesmen, would let the boys win—after a challenging fight, nonetheless—and then after each boy won, the man would remove the mask from his face and place it over the boy's face. This experience of initiation was a symbolic moment in which the boy became a man. The tribe now viewed the boy as a man: he had earned the work that came along with his role and was gifted secrets of the tribe.

From that initiation forward, the once boy now walked the world as a man. As a carrier of the secrets of the community, he assumed a vital role within the tribe, often as a hunter. The freshly initiated man had entered a new season of life. Like a snake, he had shed the former skin of a child and had been coated with the new skin of adulthood. His work became that of a man within the tribe. In time the young man would find where his work could be best leveraged.

However, with time naturally comes change, and sometimes that change is societal. On the horizon was the dawn of agricultural society. Hunter-gatherer societies slowly began to transition into farming societies. Anthropologists discuss various reasons for this transition, and though they are more qualified to discuss such reasons than I am, from my perspective this transition is important because of the shift in the demands of our work. We went from doing important work for fifteen to seventeen hours a week to doing important work from sunup to sundown all week. After we transitioned to this schedule of important work hours, we never looked back.

The shift from hunter-gatherer societies to farming societies unleashed prosperity and changed the dimensions of society in ways we could never have imagined. In this transition, while it seems straightforward to most, we find a hidden clue that helps us understand how we have gotten to a place where so many are willingly imprisoning themselves in jobs they don't like and forgoing work they are interested in. (According to James Suzman, recent surveys show that very few people find their work meaningful or interesting: worldwide, only 15 percent of workers are engaged in their jobs, two-thirds are not engaged, and 18 percent are actively disengaged.) A common belief is that hunter-gatherer societies lived brutal and stressful lives and that it was the development of farming that aided in developing a civilized society. However, anthropologists tell a different story, the story of how we experience time. In reality, hunter-gatherer societies worked fifteen to seventeen hours per week and spent the rest of their time resting and in leisure, while farming societies worked for most of the day and leisure time was, well, sleep. The transition from hunting and gathering to farming was a change of mindset, from abundance to scarcity.

The new farming society operated from a mindset of scarcity, from the perspective of being vulnerable to one's environment. Poor weather and intruders could ruin a farmer's harvest, so over time, farmers learned to prepare and plan for the worst: droughts, heavy rainfall, wild animals, and so on. Meanwhile, in hunter-gatherer societies, individuals felt the land they lived on provided consistently and with abundance, and they never took more than they needed. The difference in mindset is not trivial.

Today's modern individual continues to operate with the scarcity mindset, far removed from the abundance mindset of our hunter-gatherer ancestors. And try explaining to an Aboriginal tribe today that a group of guys from New York are paying top dollar to take a trip into the woods to hunt for leisure, as a vacation, for fun. They will ask, Is it because they need food? Nope. For clothing? Nope. For initiation? Nope, just for leisure. Just for the experience, the hobby.

As we know, the history of work didn't end with farming. Over the years, more change happened: we adapted as a species, learned, and developed new technologies along the way. With a reduction in war, famine, and plagues, the next great change in work was upon us: the opportunity to participate in interesting work. In the next chapter, we will explore this evolution, which is important because for the first time, some individuals had the opportunity to engage in work they were attracted to.

3
THE CRAFT ERA
AN EXPANSION OF IMPORTANT WORK

As long as creative values are in the forefront of the life task, their actualization generally coincides with a person's work. Work usually represents the area in which the individual's uniqueness stands in relation to society and thus acquire meaning and value. This meaning and value, however, is attached to the person's work as a contribution to society, not the actual occupation as such.

— VIKTOR FRANKL

As *Homo sapiens* continued to evolve, there came a point where we migrated from farms to cities. The change enabled an expansion in the design of work: it created opportunities and optionality. The dominant work design of this period continued to fall into the category of important work, but with the addition of options and opportunities, some individuals were able to pursue interesting work.

The dense population of cities presented humans with the opportunity to set up division of labor. A blacksmith could sell his product for currency or trade products with another, in the barter system. In this environment, individuals could specialize in their professional work and, if they were lucky enough, pursue work that was interesting. The caveat was that only a few could pursue interesting work; others were allocated their work based on the family they were born in. The latter system provided a sense of kinship with family as trade secrets were passed down the generations. These individuals had pride in their professional work and through that felt meaning, purpose, and fulfillment. The work everyone did in this era was important, but the opportunity for interesting work continued to expand.

As humans continued to adapt to being city creatures and engagement in interesting work expanded, we begin to see the growth of talent and professions, as well as the number of professional opportunities. Individuals could move to another city to pursue a profession of interest. Take Leonardo da Vinci, who moved from his hometown to Florence and then to Milan, all in pursuit of interesting work. Leonardo was in no way privileged; he was simply born in an era in which the professional work design enabled important and interesting work.

Leonardo's pursuit of interesting work was a hero's journey: After leaving his home to pursue his interest in art, he met his fair share of struggles. He started off barely able to read and never finished school. He struggled to finish commissioned paintings and moved around, searching for different opportunities, until finally, he sent the duke of Milan a letter requesting work. From there he began to become recognizable as the Leonardo we are familiar with today.

What is important to observe from this brief review of Leonardo is the existence of opportunity and optionality for an individual that was not born into a privileged situation. As with the story of Franco, he started off with little, but with courage, resilience, and belief in himself he was able to find interesting work. The opportunity to pursue his passions and the option to try different kinds of art were what enabled Leonardo to have such an extraordinary life, one that we still admire today. The design of work enabled Leonardo to become a heroic figure in *Homo sapiens'* history.

We see here that the opportunities and options to pursue interesting work were unquestionably growing. With the development of cities well on its way, the demand for different specialists was expanding in an unprecedented manner. The building of a church demanded all different types of specialized skills, the expansion of cities' populations demanded all different types of food and entertainment, and the reduction in famine, disease, and war (although they were still problems) provided time for individuals to focus on work that was not solely important but also interesting. It was a big moment and achievement in our history.

The things *Homo sapiens* built and created during this period were magnificent. It was a pure mix of interesting and important work that produced works of true beauty. While I make this period sound like the garden of Eden, it was not. There was much hardship, but it was an important era in terms of work design. We can clearly see that with the growth of opportunity and optionality within the work design of the era, individuals naturally pursued their interests, given the opportunity. They took chances on themselves and accepted the call to adventure by pursuing opportunities. While options for work were still relatively small, they were different enough to offer something to everyone. As we know, with too many options, we are paralyzed and struggle to choose.

This era of work design clearly did not last forever. With time, things change. We evolved, and with that change, the design of work began to shift again. Except this time the shift was away from important and interesting work to something totally different. While *different* doesn't always mean *bad*, the change in work was one that altered our mindset and relationship with work in a way we had never experienced before.

Was this transition necessary in order to elevate *Homo sapiens* to a better place? From my perspective, it often seems a case of one step forward, two steps back. Unfortunately, this was a time when we sacrificed our relationship to work, and over time we have gotten so far away from the original meaning of work that our former bond with our work is one that the modern individual would hardly recognize.

4
STRUCTURED WORK
THE DEATH OF IMPORTANT WORK

This is the result of having a job. One lives with such fear of losing it, that the thought of venturing outside its confines seems an impossibility.

— VICTOR D'ARGENT

Every so often, changes in an era heavily influence the design of work, and an evolution in our work systems and relationship to work follows. As a collective, we are challenged to develop new ideas, modify the current system, and implement a new one. As with most forms of evolution, we modify and build upon the existing structures; we do not start from scratch.

It would be foolish and absurd to think that we know everything that influences the changing of an era. Odds are that something influential has been overlooked or not yet realized. However, if we look back, we can identify a few vital elements, such as innovation and technology, that provided the opportunity for this new era of work, also known as the Industrial Revolution. The soil of society was turned and fertilized, primed for the boom of structured professional work.

The 1890s mark a final turning point, the period of transition where our work design shifted from that of important work with some opportunities for interesting work to that of structured work. The decades prior to the transition were tough ones, to say the least: war, the Long Depression, and Red Scare protests, such as the Haymarket Affair—a stretch of unbelievably challenging times to not only live in but survive. Luckily, society was heroic and persevered, although the scars and the wounds of the experience remain. With the dark times, our attitude and relationship to work shifted and that was the price to be paid. We were no longer in pursuit of work that was interesting or required to engage in important work; instead we desired work that provided security or, in other words, safety. A completely understandable position to take and attitude to have, given the situation and the difficulty of the past.

The collective was physically and emotionally tired, yet eager for a better life. History shows that famine, war, and disease are barriers for civilization to prosper. However, when the time arrived that the three were not pervasive within society, the collective soul was primed for the opportunity to chase prosperity.

It was the idea of scientifically managing labor that sparked the change in work design. Of course, using people to work different jobs was not a new concept to anyone in the nineteenth century, nor did it become more valuable to the collective. What changed was the design of work, and then our attitude, which influenced our relationship with work. The design change that altered professional work greatly was the way we began to leverage time.

In the design of important and interesting work, time serves as a tool, whereas in the structured and safe work design, time serves as a creative constraint. The name of the game in the industrial era was efficiency, and that demanded a simple and standardized people strategy. To gain efficiency, a level of individuality must be sacrificed. The philosophy is system first, people second. In other words, design the system to be as robust and efficient as possible, so the people operate the tasks of the system—nothing more, nothing less. The shift in work design created a radically different system. Whether this was for the betterment of society or not is subjective—although history shows this change brought great prosperity, enhancing the collective standard of living.

The change in work design demanded society modify some of the ways in which individuals and organizations worked together. In the previous era, people worked directly with each other. In the industrial era, individuals worked with companies. The change in relationship from human to human, to human to company is no small shift. When we wear the company hat, we operate differently from when we wear our own hat. This shift forever changed our relationship and attitude toward professional work.

Additionally, the work environment shifted. Originally, work was commonly done in the environments and communities of the professional. Think of an artist in their workshop, or a group of artists working together in Florence during the Renaissance. The environment then was one of community and shared inspiration. During the Industrial Revolution, work transitioned to taking place in factories, a vastly different environment. The change in environment characterized the structured work design; the objective was efficiency through intelligent systems. This change in design sought to eliminate individuality in work, and as a consequence relied on financial incentives as motivation.

It is hard to argue that the design of structured work is not useful: it created unprecedented levels of efficiency. The structured work design empowered the Industrial Revolution to achieve greater production, more consistency, and, on average, better quality.

In the beginning, it was common for most factories to manage their people based on rules of thumb, unofficial apprenticeships, and the talents and hard work of a few individuals. In other words, the people strategy was to find one skilled individual and build around them.

Factories created a slew of novel problems for the businessman and factory owner of the industrial era. The Goliath of problems—no different from today—was rooted in people strategy and management. Specifically, factories created the requirement to employ large numbers of workers. Most factory owners were not well versed in how to create people systems that enabled cooperation. Instead, factories' people strategies were calibrated toward individual output, a natural hangover from the previous era. However, that quickly proved to be a low-grade strategy. Structured work design provided a basis for leveraging the power of a group rather than an individual's ability to produce. It was inspired by the idea that the sum of the group is greater than its individual parts.

In time, factories became increasingly chaotic with the expansion of labor demands and without any clear system to manage them. The industrial era yearned for a functional people system, one that allowed workers and companies to work in harmony with one another. Part of the change had resulted from the way the individual worked. Previously, the individual (craftsman) worked at his own pace, in his own way, and had a ceiling on the volume they could produce—which often resulted in costly products and services. With innovation and technology, factories now offered individuals machines for which no apprenticeship, specialization, or years of experience in craftmanship was required. Instead, a simple, repetitive, and efficient operation was outlined and then taught to workers. They were educated on how to operate the machine and complete the task with the new structured design of work. In a way, this was the death of important and interesting work and the birth of structured and safe work. The birth of this new work design created an opportunity for the collective to engage in work that would allow them to provide for themselves and their families. In other words, it offered them security and safety. It was a work design that was built for the collective and not the individual.

At this point, the three-headed monster—war, famine, and disease—had been controlled to a point where the framework of society and work could evolve. Part of the evolution was a change in where humans lived, a migration from rural areas to urban areas. Society went from an agrarian economy to a manufacturing economy, where products were no longer made solely by hand but by machines. A change of this magnitude heavily modified the social environment, the collective culture, and individuals' relationship to work.

The new work design came with a price: our relationship to work. We slowly began losing touch with what professional work means to us as human beings and with how we experience our lives. In the structured work design, purpose, fulfillment, and meaning could no longer be important elements. Instead, the elements of efficiency, simplification, standardization, and routinization were now priority. The greatest loss in our relationship with professional work is that of acknowledging its importance to us as individuals. For example, the Spartans' mindset and their relationship to their professional work is something we rarely see today: one in which the professional work they do expresses itself in every essence of their being.

In the movie *300*, Gerard Butler plays a Spartan king who meets up with an ally army in his quest to battle the great Persian empire. The king of the ally army, surprised by the Spartan king's decision to bring "only" three hundred soldiers, makes a comment to the Spartan king regarding his failure to plan accordingly. The Spartan king responds by pointing at different soldiers in the ally army, asking the following question: "What is your profession?" One answers "I am a potter"; another says "a sculptor"; another says "a blacksmith." The Spartan king takes a moment and turns to his army and asks, "Spartans, what is your profession?" At this, the entire army, in one cadence, responds *whooooooooh, whooooooh, whooooh*, raising their spears in the air. The Spartan king ends the scene wittily, with a final remark to the ally king: "See, old friend, I brought more soldiers than you did." To the city of Sparta, you were not *sometimes* a Spartan soldier; you were a Spartan soldier in every moment of life. In that culture, "What is your profession?" was the same as asking "Who are you?"

The shift from important and interesting work design to structured and safe work design can easily be viewed as negative. However, there are many aspects to be appreciated. It's best we view these not as better or as worse, but instead as a game of trade-offs. It is imperative we remember the context of the times, the situation, and the culture of the world: safety and structure are understandable targets to pursue after much time in chaos.

With change, chaos follows, and with chaos there is great opportunity. The challenge is that the opportunities are hidden, and it takes a courageous individual to venture into the depths of chaos to find them. One man in particular clearly saw the opportunity in the chaos. His name was Frederick Taylor, and he would be both the angel and the devil of the era—a heroic villain.

PART 2
STRUCTURED & SAFE WORK

You can't use an old map to explore a new world.

— ALBERT EINSTEIN

5
A HEROIC VILLAIN

Those who misunderstand a hero see a villain.

— UNKNOWN

The story begins in the 1860s with a young boy named Frederick who by nature was analytical, something that would instinctively motivate him to create systems. Take, for example, his style of playing croquet: he would pay close attention to the details of the stroke angles to calculate the advantages of an understroke. Or at the ripe age of thirteen, when he went on a European expedition, he filled his notebooks with the most unusual of subjects, such as details on the methods for extracting salt from underwater lakes. No matter the game or the environment Frederick analyzed, the system was part of who he was, his nature.

Naturally, we can assume that having an analytical and structure-driven mind did not always make Frederick popular among other young boys, who enjoyed the chaos of childhood. While his analytical mind developed, his social skills went into debt, as there is always a cost to be paid for the acquisition of something valuable.

The curious, analytical, and system-driven boy would unknowingly begin his quest to developing labor principles that we continue to leverage today, over one hundred years later. The journey was a heroic one, although it's rarely recalled that way. The quest demanded great sacrifices along with uncomfortable struggles, but in the end, the principles developed would contribute to elevating the standard of living to the highest the world had ever seen at that time.

So Frederick matured into a man who was not well liked in his era, nor very much in modern times either. A quick perusal of popular literature that discusses his labor principles portray them (and sometimes him) in a negative light. The layperson of today who is familiar with his principles views him more as a villain than as a hero. While the labor principles Frederick developed are far from perfect, they unquestionably are a great asset for society. They unlocked doors but, more important, created windows of opportunity, and it is that latter that led to prosperity for the collective.

The analytical boy who grew up to develop labor-changing principles is none other than Frederick Winslow Taylor. His labor principles are known as the principles of scientific management, task management, or Taylorism. Taylor's ideas and principles aided the great societal transition from craft to industry and the elevation of the collective American standard of living.

Frederick's motivation was not fame, fortune, or power but frustration with the wasted potential of human beings.

He saw the labor systems in the country as a serious issue: "our larger wastes of human effort, which go on every day through such of our acts as are blundering, ill-directed, or inefficient." Frederick thought highly of human beings' capabilities and felt called to develop a labor system in which workers were motivated to provide a fair day of work, earn premium compensation, and have an opportunity for prosperity.

The aversion Frederick had toward individuals wasting their potential was far from new, as he came from an aristocratic family. He grew up watching his father participate in leisure activities appropriate for a "gentleman," such as learning foreign languages and engaging in research. These were activities that Frederick would learn to reject, as his nature was more connected with that of his maternal grandfather, who was an entrepreneur and adventurer. As Frederick's career progressed, there was even something of a maniacal, all-or-nothing compulsiveness in the way in which he pursued his vocation.

Frederick understood that the challenges for independent craftsmen at the time were production and resources. Factories provided individuals with resources and machines to produce items at a scale and at a cost that had been impossible in the previous era. The change flipped society on its head from craftsman driven to industrial driven. Frederick was inspired to find ways in which the change could be positive for both organization and individual. His principles highlight the importance of aligning talent with opportunity, as Frederick believed that "the search for better, for more competent men from the presidents of our great companies, down to the household servants, was never more vigorous than it is now."

The principles of scientific management did introduce a

power hierarchy, and with that hierarchy came a transfer of power. At the time, the workers held a majority of the power, as management was not skilled enough to truly hold the workman accountable to real quotas or expectations. The implementation of Frederick's principles provided management with a benchmark number; in turn, the workman relinquished some of his power, which transitioned to management. Frederick realized this and acknowledged that men of high character must attain the newly created positions of power for the principles to be effective, as well as that highly competent employees required premium pay. Workers and management were expected to collaborate to continuously improve the system. Unfortunately, these vital steps were not closely adhered to, which led to the principles being unintelligently administered and overwhelmingly misunderstood.

The principles of scientific management are still the framework of our people strategies today, although they have been altered in many places to fit modern times. Frederick's principles are a robust system, a genius piece of work that brought light to darkness. The change that accompanied a transitional period (craftsman to industrial) offered great opportunity for the collective. The principles of scientific management provided a framework that individuals and companies could leverage to grasp the opportunity in front of them. Those who applied the principles honestly benefited greatly, and unfortunately, those who didn't honestly apply them benefited a little as well by taking advantage of workers. A costly price of the principles was the elimination of individualism, which made changing workers an issue of logistics rather than one of talent.

The principles of scientific management were not

designed with poor intent or by an individual who was evil. They were designed to solve novel challenges and offer an opportunity for prosperity for all. However, as we all know, everything comes with a price, and the price paid for this new structured work was individuality, and this impacted our ability to have a relationship with our work. This may have been unavoidable because as we transitioned from important work to structured work, our responsibility to provide and survive remained.

Taylor designed principles that enabled everyone to provide and survive in a prosperous way. To reignite our relationship to work, we must understand why he designed the principles as he did, and the lessons we can learn when we redesign work moving forward.

6

FREDERICK'S JOURNEY
A PROFESSIONAL ADVENTURE

Only those who attempt the absurd will achieve the impossible.

— M.C ESCHER

Developing the scientific principles was a thirty-year adventure for Frederick, who traveled around the country studying organizations. He focused on understanding their work tasks systematically at a micro level to figure out the one "right" way to design a labor system that was efficient and effective. However, let's not confuse this with what Frederick thought the principal responsibility of management was, which is to secure the maximum prosperity for the employer coupled with the maximum prosperity for each employee.

Frederick outlined "maximum prosperity" for organizations as defined by large dividends for the company or owner and development of every branch of business to its highest state of excellence, so that prosperity can be permanent. For the employee, he defined it as higher wages than are usually received by men of that employee's class and development of each man to his state of maximum efficiency, so he can do the highest grade of work for which his natural abilities fit him; this meant giving him, when possible, this class of work to do.

At the beginning of the industrial era, the worker retained a disproportionate amount of power and influence. The initial factory-labor work design did not enable individuals to work hard, so they didn't. The relationship between organization and worker was hostile. Frederick questioned whether this was necessary and set out to design a system in which the worker and organization could prosper together, a positive-sum outcome instead of a zero-sum outcome. At heart, the motivation of the principles of scientific management lies in Frederick's low tolerance for the waste of human potential and his belief that by working together, the company and individual could both find success.

"Initiative-and-incentive" was the original labor-management system of factories and was not designed to develop talent or reward top talent, just to produce units. In other words, the system was simply a transaction where the worker gave their "best" initiative and in turn received some "special" incentives from their employer. It was a disorganized structured work design. The labor system of this type relied purely on the efforts of the worker, while the efforts of management were not of equal value and did not enhance output. Management seemed to take up space without really furthering the company objectives.

All quality relationships are built on fair exchange and

reciprocity. Without these, the relationship doesn't reach its potential and is not one of peace but is rather constantly on the brink of war. Factory owners were attempting to foster fair exchange with workers through a labor design referred to as "piecework"—an initiative-and-incentive methodology. Piecework is a straightforward and transparent system where a worker is paid based on production (pieces produced) and not by hours. The unit-piecework price was calculated and agreed upon beforehand.

Unfortunately, factory owners and management began to breach the piecework contract. Management would monitor the output of workers and take note of what production levels were possible, so whenever a worker came in and worked very hard, motivated by the potential of high pay, management would see a production benchmark. The next day management would alter the piece rate to a lower amount. In management's eyes, this amounted to paying the workers a fair rate. Clearly, this did not sit well with the workers: regardless of the domain, a breach of contract results in a loss of trust in any relationship. Understandably, workers took the violation of contract personally, and the relationship between workers and management took a turn for the worst.

Logically, the workers responded to management's foul play by benchmarking themselves. Thus came the introduction of soldiering, or underworking: that is, deliberately working slowly to avoid doing a full day's work. Soldiering was a conscious effort by the workers to counter management's reduction in pay (a.k.a. rate busting) with expectations of more work. Management was treating workers unfairly, so workers returned the favor. Through soldiering, workers regained control of the quotas.

However, controlling the quota was effective only if the workers banded together and no one exceeded the workman's quota. It was an all-or-nothing strategy. The culture of the workmen became one of soldiering enforcement. New workers were taught the soldiering ways, and if they did not follow them, they felt the social pressure of the group. In a way, workers were spending their time designing a system that was exactly opposite of what companies were trying to build. Soldiering was not restricted to the domain of factories but became pervasive within the collective work culture. Interestingly enough, America is the exact opposite today: we have a work-hard, make-something-of-yourself culture where nothing is standing in your way but you. Frederick is responsible for building some of this mentality.

Within the system of piecework (a.k.a. "initiative-and-incentive management"), top workers were drowned out among the mass of below-average workers. There were no incentives for top workers to produce, and in many companies, individuals were forced by the collective to limit their production. Soldiering truly became a systemic problem. Golf caddies were even instructed to purposely walk slower, as they got paid hourly, and if one did not abide by this rule, the other caddies would give him a licking. The culture of this era was becoming one of "milking the clock." Frederick witnessed and experienced the pervasive culture of soldiering firsthand when he worked at Midvale Steel, during the period when he formed his principles. He saw soldiering as the greatest evil among the working people of both England and America.

At Midvale, Frederick started out as a laborer because mechanic jobs were few and far between. Fortunately for him, the mistake of another workman quickly provided him with an opportunity. Soon after Frederick began working at the Midvale shop, his direct clerk was caught stealing, and Frederick was selected to take his place simply out of necessity. He was the next most educated individual in the group, and because of that he was given the position of clerk—Frederick was well educated for his time, even having been accepted into Harvard.

In his new position as clerk, Frederick began running his own lathe and produced more than other machinists were doing on similar lathes. Of course, this didn't go unnoticed, and once again, rather quickly, he received another promotion, becoming gang boss, overseeing the lathe. After showcasing his ability to improve lathe operations, he was promoted again, to foreman.

Frederick's formative period as a laborer proved to be an indispensable experience, as it brought him up close and personal with the practice of soldiering. It is easy to see why he felt that the collective worker culture was one that was interested not in working but instead in just coasting. He also truthfully admitted that the design of piecework was set up in a way that he understood why workmen soldiered. In other words, the dishonest work design of the piecework system manifested the response of soldiering. The clash of factory management with workers proved to limit production to about one-third of a "good day's" work. Every new workman who came into the shop was told at once by the other men exactly how much of each kind of work he was to do, and unless he obeyed these instructions, he would be driven out of the factory by the other workmen.

The pervasive culture of soldiering frustrated Frederick: he felt it was limiting the new opportunity for prosperity that the industrial era offered. But he also recognized that the lack of trust did not encourage employee and employer to be peaceful with one another but instead instigated war. Let's also not forget that Frederick's nature, from when he had been a young child, was one of analysis and system building. It was obvious to him that the design of piece-work management was fragile and ineffective, an unfit system for factories, especially with the culture of "rate busting."

Once Frederick earned the position of foreman and the trust of ownership, he began to experiment in pursuit of designing a better labor system. Because it utilized every-thing he had learned as an apprentice, laborer, and manager, as well as his talents, it was a fitting and inspiring problem for Frederick, one that he was extremely interested in. The approach was simple: design a system where workers and employees have a fair exchange and in which employers offer labor premium pay for a fair day of work, eliminating workers' motivation to soldier.

Frederick viewed soldiering as something that was predominantly a communication problem and believed much of this stemmed from the fact that there was no benchmark for what constituted a "fair day's work." How could employer and employee engage in fair exchange if a fair day of work was not clear? While a foreman, he began experimenting to figure out what a fair day of work might be, but within the confines of the piecework system. It proved to be an impossible task; he struggled to motivate or incentivize the workmen to produce any more than they had previously done. No matter the threats or opportuni-ties offered, the workmen would not budge. Frustrations grew, and the relationship between Frederick and the workmen became hostile.

Frederick decided to take a different approach and

began hiring green workmen, training them himself, paying them above market value, and providing financial incentives for hitting production quotas, which were labeled a fair day's work. After he had done this a few times, the culture of the shop began to change: some workmen adopted the new ways, and others were forced out. Frederick was beginning to shape the principles of scientific management, a needed replacement for piecework.

After about five years, Midvale was operating more efficiently and producing more than ever. However, Frederick still believed that without complete clarity about what constituted a fair day's work, it would be a challenge for employers and employees to cooperate. Because of Frederick's track record, ownership at Midvale trusted him and gave him the green light to conduct research experiments, introducing science, even though they didn't see the value in it. This was a vital moment in work design history: without freedom to experiment, Frederick would never have created the principles of scientific management. Immediately, he began conducting time and motion studies.

Time and motion studies proved to be the main tool for the design of the principles of scientific management. Simply put, time and motion broke down every job into a list of tasks, measured how long each task took, and reviewed whether it could be improved upon with modifications to the process, whether that be changing the tools, using the tools in a different way, changing how the process was organized, or altering the layout of the factory. The studies generally produced options for greater efficiency. Time and motion studies introduced science to the design of work.

With the findings from time and motion studies, Frederick began to make bigger changes at Midvale. Most were met with resistance; nonetheless, they were effective. Midvale management's trust in Frederick grew, though only at the price of his shattered relationships with the workmen who were once his comrades. The tension is understandable, as the level of change was great, and change naturally introduces some chaos, creating tension and stress. However, the changes Frederick implemented were rooted in fair exchange so that employer and employee would both prosper. Because the new labor system was designed to eliminate soldiering, it's natural that many did not like it, especially given the culture of the time. The principles of scientific management were the opposite of what workers were used to. Even though the change was intended for the honest good of both parties, seeing its validity required time.

The introduction of science to the design of work proved to crystallize the principles. Much of what Frederick seemed to intuitively know or had figured out from his variety of jobs was now supported with scientific evidence and was given a framework—the principles of scientific management. Frederick committed his professional life to developing and critiquing this system, by which organizations and individuals could work together to prosper. But more important, his was a design in which labor and its development became essential elements. It was a system built upon fair exchange, best-in-class processes that produced efficiency and quality, and, most important, the intelligent selection of individuals for work.

The changing of the era created great opportunities, but it was not obvious how to recognize them or act upon them. Change is hard and uncomfortable, especially at the magnitude called for by the shift from important and interesting work design to structured and safe work. Frederick leveraged the tools of science to make sense of the chaos and to provide companies and individuals the blueprint to work together fairly and peacefully. He believed that the old design relied too much on one perfect employee to be the hero, instead of using the collective abilities of all the employees. Frederick understood the work environment had changed with the introduction of factories and that individuals were now working in larger groups. Clearly this required a system in which fair exchange was easy and transparent.

The addition of larger groups of workers also created a responsibility to train these individuals, something that Frederick saw as a great opportunity. However, to train these individuals, management needed to know the best way to conduct each task and then develop a training system around it. The insights provided by science and the art of the task were what led to the cooperation between management and employee, one that was missing in the piecework system. Management brought the science, and employees brought the task knowledge (or art), and together they figured out what was the most effective and efficient design. This principle was critical in retaining the skills and talents of the top workers.

Working together in this way fashioned trust and friendship between management and employees, something Frederick felt was missing in work society and which was a necessity for the principles to be successful. Impressively enough, over the thirty years during which Frederick and his team implemented the principles, there was not one strike or fight between employees and companies.

The hallmark of the principles of scientific management

is fair exchange. Unfortunately, what we find in many discussions of Frederick and his principles is bitterness between labor and management. The principles laid forth were interpreted in a way that portrayed Frederick as someone who separated workers from the greater meaning of their work and his principles as dehumanizing, leading to deskilling of individuals, which made them expendable, and creating repetitive work tasks that caused mental anguish for workers and led to worker burnout. In most cases, he is viewed as the villain, and we point our finger at him for many of the tensions we feel today between companies and individuals.

If we read his book *The Principles of Scientific Management* with an open eye and with understanding of the context of the work design, it's hard to imagine that Frederick was anything but a hero. In no way were the principles perfect or free from error, but they were invaluable in a time of massive change during which human potential was being wasted.

Nonetheless, not many men in Frederick's position would have had the courage to act and continue to act. Frederick came from an affluent family; he did not need to choose the more difficult work journey. But then he would not have developed principles that are still utilized today. He paved his own path, something that was relatively rare, as it still is today.

There is no doubt that Frederick's family aided in providing opportunities, experience, and education. It would be silly to ignore this and what it means in relation to the culture of his time. However, Frederick worked obsessively in developing his principles. This is a mentality that is respected in America today: a spirit of relentlessness, a courageous pursuit of a worthwhile purpose. The modern worker who engages in interesting work draws on the culture Frederick, with his unique personality, did much to create, which is the opposite of what the collective work culture was at the beginning of the Industrial Revolution.

Frederick experienced threats from individuals who one day were his friends and then the next became enemies. The turmoil between workers and management was far from comfortable, and it was something that Frederick did not enjoy; neither did he believe it was any way to live life. In his own words, "For any right-minded man, however, this success is in no sense a recompense for the bitter relations which he is forced to maintain with all those around him. Life that is one continuous struggle with other men is hardly worth living."

Frederick provided us with the springboard needed to restructure the relationships between organizations and individuals to be based on shared interest instead of antagonism. Working together provided the opportunity to mass-produce products at prices that could be affordable to the collective, thus enhancing the standard of living for everyone. Henry Ford leveraged these principles to make a car that was affordable for everyone. Today, Elon Musk is applying the same principles, but in a modern way, to mass-produce electric cars and rockets.

Frederick developed his framework during a moment of great change, when a new way of work design was desperately needed. The principles were not based solely on profitability but on developing a way to incentivize individuals to be their best and to reward them when the agreed-upon task was accomplished. It was a system based on cooperation and the idea of companies and individuals working together as allies, not enemies. If the principles were followed honestly and diligently, then growth and profit were all but guaranteed, for both the individual and the company.

The industrial era increased the demand for competent workers to a point that clearly exceeded the available supply—which was not a reflection of workers' capabilities but of the relationship between employer and employee. Frederick knew firsthand there was a better way, one in which both worker and manager could prosper together, as they depended on each other like never before.

Frederick saw the scientific management principles as something that could be applied with equal force to all social activities: the management of our homes, the management of our farms, the management of the businesses of tradespeople (large and small)—as well as our churches, our philanthropic institutions, our universities, and our governmental departments. Over one hundred years later, the principles of scientific management continue to be the framework of our labor ecosystem and are pervasive in most companies, although one thing remains consistent from when Frederick first released these principles in 1919 till today: many don't read the fine print and misunderstand them. Therefore, the principles are misused, and Frederick is labeled a villain.

Ultimately, Frederick's principles have become the rules and outlines for the design of structured and safe work. If we are to adjust our attitude toward work, we first need to understand the underlying game that continues to influence work today so we can modify and modernize the design. To a master, rules and principles provide opportunity for creativity; for the novice, they are barriers and mines—two vastly different perspectives and attitudes. A chess master leverages the rules of chess, while the novice chess player is held captive by them. Modern individuals (and companies) are imprisoned by the misunderstandings and outdated ideas of structured and safe work design. To adopt a different mindset for professional work, we first must find clarity regarding the principles that are the foundation of work design today.

7
THE PRINCIPLES

Knowledge is knowing that a tomato is fruit. Wisdom is knowing not to put a tomato in a fruit salad.

— MARTIN JOHNSON

Most literature about the principles of scientific management and Frederick Winslow Taylor is far from positioning them in a positive light. Quotes and ideas from *The Principles of Scientific Management* are taken out of context, leading the reader to believe the principles are appalling and almost criminal. Yet the common work design of today, structured and safe work, depends on Frederick's principles, although they are rarely understood, appreciated, or discussed.

Some of Frederick's motivation for designing the principles came from his innate desire to help society prosper and to eliminate the waste of human potential, as exemplified by soldiering. To him, this was best done with efficient production, high wages, and low labor costs, something that doesn't, at first glance, seem to make sense. However, we must remember how things were done prior to the Industrial Revolution and the introduction of structured work. In that time, most items were created by hand and tool, limiting the number that could be produced, thus driving up the price. For example, when shoes went from being made by hand to being produced in factories, the transition completely changed the shoe market and the wider culture. Previously, going barefoot had been normal among the common people. Most wore shoes for special occasions, and most could afford to buy them only every few years. Once shoes were produced in factories, the cost of shoes was reduced to the point where individuals could buy them more often, encouraging people to start wearing them daily. Naturally, this increased the demand for shoes, which increased the opportunity for shoe labor.

To Frederick, this capitalistic cycle was obvious and presented great opportunity. He wasn't alone in thinking this, because in 1908 a man named Henry Ford developed the first affordable car—in any color you wanted, as long as it was black. This affordable car changed society in ways we can never totally appreciate, and it was all made possible by Frederick's principles. The principles of scientific management yielded great results when workers were not soldiering, jobs were designed in a scientific manner, and employers and employees engaged in a cooperative relationship that was rooted in trust and fair exchange, each pulling their weight to help the other prosper.

The fundamental goal of managing people with the scientific principles was to eliminate the motivation for soldiering, which Frederick thought was pervasive in the work culture. As long as soldiering was prevalent among the workers, inefficiencies and wasted human effort would be the norm.

There were three main drivers of soldiering. First, the workers of Frederick's era deeply believed the fallacy that increased output would lead to mass unemployment. Second, the current labor system, piecework, was unjust and encouraged the workman to soldier to protect his best interest. Third, common rules of thumb that workers applied did not lead to efficiency or effective production in the environment of a factory. Frederick's principles were developed to combat these variables.

There is no question that the language Frederick uses is at times harsh, but this also can be read as a reflection of passion and conviction. His interest was to help develop structures, to find organization in chaos, to see things that were not obvious to the unobservant. It just so happened that he directed this energy and talent toward designing a structured work system to solve the challenge of managing people, one meant to help bring peace in the war between workers and managers.

The problem Frederick was committed to solving was efficiency, but as an overall philosophy, his principles were about society prospering. The lack of people strategy was inhibiting the collective from capitalizing on the opportunity the Industrial Revolution provided. Frederick recognized this and offered the principles of scientific management as a solution.

Now that we have clarity about the history, context, and motivations behind Frederick's ideas, we can better understand the foundation of the structured and safe work design and further explore the principles of scientific management. There are four of them: job design, labor selection, cooperation, and fair exchange.

PRINCIPLE #1: SCIENTIFIC JOB DESIGN

Objective: Develop a science for each element of a job, which replaces the old rule-of-thumb method.

The status quo for professional workers prior to the Industrial Revolution was to conduct their professional work how they saw fit. Individuals learned their work from others and by leveraging rules of thumb. Some work domains had official apprenticeships and others a more learn-on-the-job philosophy. Frederick appreciated the value of apprenticeships and learning on the job but saw a lack of consistency across the board: if everyone completed a job or task differently, then it would be almost impossible to work as a team. Going from independent to collective necessitates a different working mindset, from finishing the job to finishing a part of the job, a task.

The first principle of scientific management was not new to individuals or societies; it was the introduction of science to it that gave it a different flavor. In its simplest form, it's structured division of labor.

The innovation of machines and technology during the industrial era provided the chance to develop widgets at a quicker rate and cheaper price. Frederick's principle of job design was a way to leverage or aggregate the best rules of thumb and then stress test them with time and motion studies. It identified the rules of thumb that were effective and the ones that were not. The measurement of effectiveness was speed. Efficiency was the goal. The objective of the experiments was to intelligently simplify the design of a job and benchmark a fair day's work.

Contrary to the belief that Frederick wanted to work the individual to death, he in fact wanted to work individuals to the perfect point at which they could come back the next day and have the same output. Consistency and reliability were what Taylor was after. Efficiency was the goal. There is no value in burning out people when you have already invested time in selecting and training them. The principles of scientific management clearly note the importance of avoiding labor burnout.

The development of simplified jobs aided in clarifying expectations between management and workers, creating clear and transparent lines for division of labor. For fair exchange to be possible, both parties need to have an idea of what each expects of the other. The clarity of jobs was to help workers and management hold each other account-able. Without clarity of expectations, we see that manage-ment and workers struggled to work in harmony together.

A key component in the transition of the Industrial Revolution was the number of individuals who would be working together. Organizing five hundred to a thousand individuals is no easy task today, despite our technology and understanding of human beings. A hundred years ago, it was a serious challenge, one that was far beyond the abil-ities of most factory owners. Part of scientific job design was creating a structure and framework in which a large group of workers could be connected as well as focused on their tasks. The shift in mentality was challenging because industrial work itself was something that few find mean-ing, purpose, fulfillment, or interest in. But most of all, people were working next to each other, not necessarily with each other. This is a noteworthy shift from important and interesting work design to structured and safe work design.

In important and interesting work design, there is still some structure; it's valuable. The use of structure in important and interesting work design is driven by necessity of the work. A group of hunters have a strategy in how they hunt, a structure to the hunt; it allows them to hunt as a team, a unit. This is no different from being in an army or on a basketball team. Without some structure we operate in chaos. The work is too important, so we need to work in teams, not groups, to have the optimal chance of success. There is a difference between teams and groups. A team consists of individuals who work together in pursuit of something that they believe is bigger than themselves. A group consists of people who work for themselves on something that they may or may not believe in, care about, or have interest in. The design of structured and safe work makes building teams very hard, so most default to building groups of workers.

Part of our disconnected relationship with professional work came with this change to design work based on efficiency. The shift in mentality made factory work a game driven by process design, in which the measure of success was efficiency and profit. If jobs were intelligently designed, then management could begin to truly manage and cooperate with workers.

The principle of scientific job design is related to the idea that the whole is greater than the sum of its parts. Putting the system first and people second was Frederick's brash way of saying the same thing. It's clear that human beings are not the biggest or strongest form of life on earth; instead, our survival as a species is deeply rooted in our ability to cooperate. Our ability to hunt together and then share our kill is built into us from the time of our earliest ancestors. Our very nature is social; there is no debate about this.

If we are to do great work, there comes a moment when division of labor is inevitable. Division of labor aids in making professional work efficient, and that matters. However, there is a line, and if efficiency is the sole goal, we cross the line to sacrificing individuality. This type of professional work is designed so that everyone works the exact same way, at the exact same time. There is no room for an individual to express themselves in their professional work. Everyone strictly follows the paved path; any deviation means the efficiency of the system is at risk. With structured and safe work design, it's hard for individuals to maintain any connection with their professional work, and it becomes a mere job.

Job design is not a new concept to civilization or humans. It's essentially the concept of the division of labor, just with the addition of science. Division of labor has been enacted intuitively over thousands of years, but the addition of science—specifically time and motion studies—had a great impact. In one way, it broke the connection between individuals and their professional work; in another way, it provided opportunities to the collective, who desperately needed them.

There are only so many individuals who have the skills to independently make something that is valuable for society. On the flip side, there are a vast number of individuals who have skills that, when partnered with complementary skills, can produce value for the society as a collective. Job design enhanced the collective's talents, contrary to the common belief that it deskilled the workforce. Designing work in a way that the collective does not rely on the rare talents of one person is valuable. A work design that trains individuals and provides clarity in expectations and the opportunity to earn premium pay is simple in theory but was an unusual concept at the time.

The benefit of over one hundred years of scientific job design is that we have gone through a variety of job design iterations. The drawback of heavily leaning on scientific job design is that the idea of "one best way" is limiting, due to the simple fact that not all professional work values efficiency, and efficiency is what lies at the heart of scientific job design.

For professional work to reach new levels, work design needs to allow for individuality. If work is designed in such a way that individuals can't express themselves in it, it suffocates the opportunity to progress the profession and discover new aspects and ways of working. We eliminate the opportunity for happy accidents.

Take this argument from Matt Ridley's *The Rational Optimist*: according to anthropologist Joe Henrich, human beings learn skills from each other by copying prestigious individuals, and they innovate by making mistakes that are very occasionally improvements—that is how culture evolves. The bigger the connected population, the more skilled the teacher, and the bigger the probability of a productive mistake. Conversely, the smaller the connected population, the greater the steady deterioration of the skill as it is passed on.

Job design still has a place in the world, but not in every professional environment. Currently it's the default for all professional environments, and it's a key element to structured and safe work design. Meanwhile, in important and interesting work design, the concept of division of labor is a key element. The concept of division of labor is fascinating;

it's a behavior we see across species. What enhances *Homo sapiens'* ability to engage in division of labor is that we have learned to practice it with strangers and on a global scale. Today companies and individuals can hire someone at the click of a button or outsource a project to a freelancer, and everything in between. Specialization, which comes from division of labor, enables great opportunity and optionality for interesting work. Friedrich Hayek called the ever-expanding possibility generated by a growing division of labor the catallaxy: something that amplifies itself once it begins.

Today we leverage job design in most professional environments. Tesla and SpaceX no doubt applied division of labor and job design principles; otherwise, building rockets and cars the way they do would be far too complicated. Applying the idea of division of labor by putting individuals in professional roles that they are well suited for and interested in, and designing a work environment they can find success in, is far from easy, but it is a nonnegotiable if you want to yield great work and positive-sum outcomes. Job design is a valuable tool to leverage in some environments, but it should no longer be the default.

However, for Frederick, job design was an essential principle, as it provided him the information to hire better. This takes us to the next principle: selection and training.

PRINCIPLE #2: SCIENTIFIC SELECTION AND TRAINING OF WORKERS

Objective: Management/ownership scientifically selects, trains, teaches, and develops the workman (whereas in the past he chose his own work and trained himself as best he could).

Naturally, as we better understand jobs and the tasks necessary to those jobs, the puzzle of selection—hiring—becomes easier. Job design was intended not only to develop an efficient way to do a job but also to benchmark what constitutes a fair day's work. While science was used to design a job, estimations of a fair day's work produced far from scientific numbers. These relied on human judgment; nonetheless, they provided a benchmark.

With an efficient process designed for each job, management could hire individuals who fit the criteria—in other words, who possessed the skills and abilities to do the job. Some industrial jobs required individuals to carry heavy pig iron, which weaker men simply could not do. Frederick himself noted that this didn't make these workers better or worse people; they were simply not qualified for that job. Hiring individuals for the jobs that they are best suited for is a challenge, no matter what domain you operate in. Frederick looked to apply science in developing the best way to do a job, which then would be the outline for training the workers. Science brought valuable clarity to the labor domain: it highlighted the essential characteristics each worker required to be considered for a job.

The sentiment of principle number two is harsh, since it ignores a person's individuality—their unique qualities—and simply looks at their skills, in a box-checking fashion, to determine whether they can or cannot do a job the way it was designed. The beneficial side of principle number two is the company's acceptance of the responsibility for training and developing the workers. Managers help the workers reach the benchmark set for production levels, and the workers want to meet the benchmark to earn the greatest financial rewards available.

Frederick pushed for a culture in which the development of individuals and their skills was pivotal, and where the responsibility of management was to ditch a sink-or-swim mentality regarding workers, replacing it with one in which if workers had the baseline criteria needed to swim, management would teach and train them to do the rest. In his own words, "What we are all looking for... is the ready-made, competent man; the man whom someone else has trained. It is only when we fully realize that our duty, as well as our opportunity, lies in systematically cooperating to train and to make this competent man, instead of hunting for a man whom someone else has trained, that we shall be on the road to national efficiency."

If we look around the world today, we still see companies practicing this idea of training and developing individuals. Take the professional soccer organization FC Barcelona. During any given year, they are considered one of the best soccer teams in the world, and they have one of the richest histories. Many of the all-time greatest soccer players have played for Barcelona; it is considered an honor to be on the team. This is very similar to the reputation of the Lakers in the NBA or the Yankees in baseball. Whether or not you are a fan of these teams, you cannot deny their heritage and history.

Barcelona has a world-class youth team development program that is an essential part of the team's consistent greatness within the soccer world. Early on, the program teaches and develops talented young players to learn the Barcelona way of playing soccer, and when they are ready

—regardless of age—they fit right into the system at the professional level. Barcelona's youth academy produced one of the greatest players, if not the greatest ever, Lionel Messi. It is hard to imagine a Messi without the guiding support and development of the Barcelona organization.

The shift in mentality to developing your people and not trying to get already-made workmen is one that seems obvious to us today but was not evident to business owners and managers before Frederick's principles advocated for it. Again, this is not a new concept to human beings. Apprenticeships and the like date back to the earliest civilizations. What was new was training and development of strangers. The labor challenge that the Industrial Revolution brought into play was that individuals who didn't really know each other were expected to work cordially and trust each other. The early factory environment—piecework management—wasn't set up for mutual respect or fair reciprocation; instead, it was set up as an us-versus-them worker-manager split. For optimal company performance, working as one unit was a necessity—what I call the Spartan mindset versus the Achilles mindset.

The Spartan mindset is one that is oriented toward important work, while an Achilles mindset is one that is oriented toward interesting work. The Spartans operated as a unit, very similar to how Frederick wished to design a factory, with the idea that the whole is more than the sum of its parts. Achilles, on the other hand, wished to become the greatest warrior that ever lived. He operated by paving his own path toward that dream and played by his own rules. Achilles operated by cultivating his own small team, and each of them fought individually.

The challenge of hiring structured work design is that maybe an individual is fit for the job but not in the structured manner it was designed to be done. As we know today, there are few arenas in which there is only one best way of doing a job. Having a framework makes sense when you expect the principles to be obeyed to a tee and when the objective is efficiency, but this suffocates innovation and workers' creativity.

Part of the criticism Frederick received for his principles was that professional work became mundane and painfully repetitive, and there is truth to that. However, without the development of workers' abilities, the factory process would never reach its efficiency potential. With each individual working differently, bottlenecks would develop in places where a worker was either new to the environment and still learning the processes or not fit for the work and in over their head. The former could be fixed with time and training, the latter by developing a new process or system. Clearly the easier route was training and development.

The collective intelligence at the time of the industrial era was not as deep or wide as it is today. Collective education during the early twentieth century was bottom heavy, with only 6 percent of the population achieving a high school diploma. Compare that with today, in which 90 percent of the population has a high school diploma. This is not a trivial point. A highly intelligent and competent workforce demands and values different things and different professional work; this is part of the challenge we face today. However, during the early twentieth century, the workforce predominantly had little education and minimal skills. Given this context, work design needed to be structured, simple, transparent, and fair and to offer opportunities for development and growth.

The principle of scientific labor selection and training supported collective development. Take the Flynn effect, which highlights the improvement in IQ scores among the least intelligent. In other words, the intelligence gap is shrinking. There will always be a gap, but its extent has been greatly reduced. The leveling up of IQ is caused by an equalization of nutrition, stimulation, and diversity of childhood experience. Structured and safe work design provided people a consistency in income. The next generation built upon this, and the ripple effect began.

Principle number two of scientific management is geared toward putting workers in structured jobs they are fit for and helping them find success in them. In a way, it was a back door to developing peaceful relationships between manager and worker so they could operate as a team and not be separated as two different tribes. Developing a labor system in which strangers can trust each other is far from easy. The true benefit, though, is passed along to members of the next generation, who are allotted the essential time to receive an education and develop as individuals—instead of school being something only the privileged experience. We must not undervalue how structured work design can bring people together and have them cooperate toward a common goal that elevates the society around them.

PRINCIPLE #3: COOPERATION

Objective: Management/ownership heartily cooperates with the men to ensure all the work is done in accordance with the scientific principles that have been developed.

Is there a difference in the relationship between worker and manager, employee and employer, labor and company, or individual and group? For any relationship to be worthwhile, beneficial, and useful to both parties, a minimum level of trust is essential. The greater the trust within a group, the greater the challenges that group can overcome, for the greatest challenges in life have a "leap of faith" aspect built into them. This depth of trust can sometimes foolishly guide a group where no sane group would go, but pushing the boundaries of the prior generation is vital to our development. The industrial era introduced many changes and new elements that had a major impact on the design of work, but none more than the relationship of the individual to their profession and workers to companies.

At the dawn of the Industrial Revolution, the relationship of the worker and the organization was not one of peace. The culture of rate busting and soldiering destroyed any possibility of collective trust for either side. The labor environment of factories was chaos. Workers and managers were all novices within their roles, although in most cases they had the skills and abilities to do the professional work. What was lacking was clarity on how to leverage machines and large groups of workers efficiently. Given the state of tension between labor and management, it didn't look like either side was working on solving it.

Cooperation is about developing trust through collaboration in navigating this new environment. The work design changed, rules of the game were altered, and collective beliefs and values evolved. The industrial era was proving to be vastly different from what had come before, and in an unpredictable way. The simplicity of principle number three lies in the idea that workers know the job best and management knows the science best, and by working together, they can develop a system that produces more with less effort for the worker, enabling companies to hit benchmarked numbers (such as profit) and workers to earn more money because the efficient system allows them to produce more in fewer hours. While this did not always happen, this was the intent of the principle of cooperation.

In a way, principle number three is simply the documented version of the player-coach relationship, the student-sensei relationship, the apprentice-artist relationship—in general, the evolution of the student under the guidance of the teacher. Frederick rightfully thought that it was impossible for any individual to do everything and to know everything—not a common belief at the time. It was better to split the work up and allow workers who are most fit to do x job to focus on doing x job, while workers who are most fit to do y job can focus on doing y job. In this model, workers not only increase production but also raise the standard of consistent quality. Once again, we hear the undertone of division of labor. While a master craftsman who operates in the interesting work design can still produce widgets of a higher quality than a team of average workers, that average team, operating in a structured work design, can produce more of that widget consistently and at a better price. The craftsmen simply cannot keep pace when it comes to widgets that have a high demand volume. However, the master craftsman is of great value in developing bespoke products for those who can afford to pay premium prices for the intricacies a master provides. The market must be primed for that product or service and have enough diversity of demand that there is a group willing to pay a premium price for x.

For example, back to shoes: they were originally crafted by hand. The time dedicated to making a pair of shoes was great, and as a result, shoes were expensive. Naturally, the price limited the number of people who could afford shoes; the demand was there, but the supply was limited. One day factories began producing shoes faster, more cheaply, and consistently, and with a better average quality. The collective naturally took a pivot to buying the cheaper, better shoe, aiding everyone—except the craftsman shoemaker. The transition in shoe manufacturing changed their cost, and they became a collective commodity instead of something affordable only to the wealthy. A collective widget, such as shoes or the affordable Model T, impacts not only our work but the culture and society of the time.

Today, we have individuals who customize shoes or produce limited editions that command an aftermarket price of ten times their value. A limited-edition shoe might hit the market at a price of $100 but then be resold for $1,000. The aftermarket shoe domain has gotten so big that many earn a living off it. To many, these shoes are pieces of art and objects to be valued as a part of an identity. We have transitioned from a time when shoes were rare and only a few people could afford them to a time when shoes are so abundant that people pay a premium for rare ones.

What is interesting about today's market is the return of the craftsman. Individual artistry has made its return, and a large part of that may be a characteristic of the era we are in. Organizations like Nike are partnering with different artists and producing limited-edition shoes and clothing. The goal is to produce quality products, but also those with a unique and artistic flavor. The beauty is in the cooperation of both sides: the science of making a shoe and the art of designing the identity of a shoe. As we look back on the history of factories, we can see that this natural progression is difficult without a starting point. The hallmark of the third principle, cooperation, is bringing individuals together and developing an atmosphere of trust so that the talents, skills, and abilities of each can be utilized to create something that would be impossible individually. It is a beautiful thing.

We see the elements of principle number three in many aspects of modern-day work because cooperation is an essential element to us as humans. Frederick didn't originate this idea, nor is he the first to discuss it. He simply was the one to acknowledge that for companies as well as individuals to prosper, cooperation is essential. Today that rings as true as it did over one hundred years ago. Cooperation between individuals is vital in all professional work, regardless of its work design. The level of cooperation can vary, but a few elements are constant: fair exchange and reciprocity.

PRINCIPLE #4: FAIR EXCHANGE

Objective: Almost equal division of the work and the responsibility between the management and the workmen. The management takes over all work for which they are better fitted than the workmen (while in the past almost all the work and the greater part of the responsibility were thrown upon the men).

In the beginning of the Industrial Revolution, managers lacked the resources or skills to truly manage people. Either they lacked familiarity with the jobs, or they lacked ability to motivate workers to do anything differently. Ultimately, managers were often simply individuals who walked around the company, adding very little value to the output of product. Meanwhile, the workers were responsible for everything: planning the work, deciding how much work should be done and how it should be done, and determining what kind of tools to use. Of course, with all the responsibilities came much of the power within the company (or factory).

Cultivating cooperation between the two parties—workers and managers—required a degree of power to be released from the workers and shared with managers. With the new acquisition of power, management was expected to work just as hard as the workers. Principle number four was about management having skin in the game and pulling its weight. It was about utilizing management's talents and skills for the overall goals of the company. For a company to maximize production and efficiencies, everyone needed to do their jobs accordingly.

For cooperation to be effective, a certain degree of trust is mandatory—something that was completely lacking in the piecework design and within the professional work design as a whole. With skin in the game, management could be held accountable, just as the workers on the floor were held accountable, each working toward the betterment of the company or factory because that would theoretically reflect the betterment of everyone.

From Frederick's perspective, management was responsible for figuring out what the best process for each task was, how to select individuals for the task, and how to set benchmarks for a fair day's work that would be accompanied by premium pay (given the benchmark was met). If individuals were not achieving a fair day's work, management's duty was to help them improve through training or other means of education. Frederick himself was not shy of jumping on a lathe and showing the workers how to do it.

One of the beneficial outcomes of the fourth principle was that when management and workers engaged in a fair and trustworthy manner, together they would continuously enhance the operations. Workers would give management feedback on what was working (and not working), and management would take that feedback to calibrate a system or process, creating a feedback loop that updated and modified the system to stay efficient as situations changed and new knowledge was acquired. Frederick himself did this throughout his entire life; he identified as a reformer. Together, management and workers could produce great things and prosper in a way where individually they would be restricted.

By working as a team in which the responsibilities were equally and effectively distributed, companies and factories found success in not only efficiency but also increased production. The company and workers both prospered. Underlying Frederick's philosophy is the goal of long-term prosperity; he purposely avoided worker burnout and strove to design a fair system. The common work design of the time, initiative and incentive, proved to be fragile as management acted more as a cheap babysitter than a valuable contributing team member.

With this ideal of reciprocity, management strives to help workers earn more money and work fewer hours, and workers strive to meet the fair day's work benchmark. There must be trust within the partnership and the exchange. Without trust, cooperation between worker and employer is merely a facade, something that both parties fake, though underneath the masks, neither is smiling. It's embodied in the saying "They pretend to pay us, and we pretend to work" (a witticism common in the USSR).

Principle number four, cooperation, provided managers a level of clarity and power that in the wrong hands could easily be manipulated. This type of transition of power was successful only when managers accepted their new power with humility, honest communication, and mature character. Unfortunately, the opposite often occurred, with management leveraging its power and insight in a hierarchal and controlling way. Surely, this was a missed opportunity for companies, leading to hostile relations instead of the desired peaceful ones.

To be clear, principle number four's theme is cooperation, but its undertone is one of bringing strangers together in a system of rules and expectations that is fair and honest and has a positive-sum outcome. An environment of this character was rare, if not nonexistent, at the time. The relationship between manager and worker was closer to that of master and slave than of two humans who respect each other and understand that the whole is greater than the sum of its parts.

The focus on cooperation between managers and workers required a heroic effort to shift the work culture of the time from one of hostility to one of harmony. When every player had skin in the game and held the idea of shared prosperity, getting a group of individuals to cooperate was far easier.

While the essence of principle four is captured by the idea of fair exchange, with everyone on the team pulling their weight and doing more together, it's easy to see how structured work design can complicate it. Such a design cultivates an attitude of coming to work, keeping one's head down, doing one's job, and going home. Nothing more, nothing less. Clearly this negatively affects our connection and relationship with our professional work.

We face similar challenges regarding fair exchange in our professional work today, as the structured work design is too rigid. What constitutes fairness seems to be contextual, not universal, and defining it entails walking that fine line between catering to individual or to collective beliefs. What is fair this year may not be next year, and what is impossible this year may be part of the status quo next year.

The key to fair exchange in professional work is honest conversation and appropriate calibration: having the courage to alter or modify terms of agreement when external or internal elements change, or new information is learned. The relationship between a company and individual is one that is in constant flux and demands attention. Principle number four, in a perfect world, encourages management to accept the responsibility of supporting the workers and to enable them to execute company objectives.

Evolving cultural values and beliefs affect what constitutes fair exchange. It's rarely easy to edit or modify professional work design to reflect these cultural changes. However, if approached heroically, challenges present opportunities and can open doors that were once locked or unattainable. Sometimes pain presents purpose. If we review the general approaches leveraged in structured work design, we can identify the areas in which context matters and the general design is not effective (or intelligent). A surface-level approach to designing fair exchange rarely works, yet a thoughtful form of reciprocation is an essential element in professional work design.

For example, imagine a company that hires a single mother and provides her the flexibility required to take care of her children, as compared with another company that does not offer this, forcing the mother to find other means to care for her children. She needs professional work to provide for her children, but her children also need their mother. A company that operates in a structured work design fails to acknowledge this simply because it fails to understand that fair exchange in one aspect of life is different from fair exchange in another. In other words, fair exchange is not identical across all conditions and all domains.

Fair exchange must be understood from a level of totality and not isolation. Structured work design looks at fair exchange separate from the rest of a person's life. Such is the challenge of the scenario of a professional working mother. In the modern era, more and more individuals will not sacrifice time with family for professional work, which was the status quo a generation ago. Fair exchange and cooperation today look vastly different than they did fifty years ago, as they should. Our professional work design needs to reflect this.

Clearly this is not rocket science, and I doubt that many people will question this thinking, but for some reason we feel compelled to continue making general processes and procedures that apply across entire companies. We forget that our season of life greatly dictates the characteristics and elements of what we deem a fair exchange.

Frederick developed an elementary fair-exchange outline that focused only on finances. At the time, money was the crucial element; people were trying to survive. However, today's world is different: individuals have the opportunity not only to survive but also to enjoy life and many of its beautiful aspects that earlier generations didn't dream of. The design of work can expand from structured to interesting. The work optionality and opportunity modern individuals have is truly a gift from the hard work of the generations before us, who didn't have much opportunity or optionality. Fair exchange and reciprocity are key elements that have been intuitively known to *Homo sapiens* from the beginning, but it's the idea of being able to achieve them with a group of strangers in a professional setting that complicates things. Chaos naturally ensues if we give general structure to these abstract agreements and don't calibrate them as our cultures change. Within the professional work domain, intelligently designing, cultivating, and maintaining fair exchange is a first-order principle.

8

UNDERAPPRECIATED

You cannot hope to make progress in areas where you have taken no action.

— EPICTETUS

Once Frederick drafted the principles of scientific management, they gained popularity and began to spread like wildfire. Unfortunately, they frequently were taken out of context, criticized, altered, and manipulated. It's foolish to critique the principles and their creator without acknowledging the faults of the individual who doesn't implement them appropriately.

The principles of scientific management gave shape to structured work design, and that no doubt helped society prosper greatly. Yet in the modern era, those same guiding principles and structured work design may be the things restricting us from a new wave of prosperity.

However, that doesn't mean we should throw out all

the principles and start over; instead, we should edit and balance the principles so we can design work in a way that reflects the modern era. We must remember that evolution is the alteration and improvement of existing systems, not the act of starting from scratch.

A common misunderstanding is that Frederick wanted individuals to work to their death and that his principles dehumanized the individual. Critics of the principles of scientific management believe they eliminated specialization among individuals, making them easily replaceable and therefore less valuable. Unfortunately, there is some truth to this. Poor leadership and management took advantage of the new clarity the principles provided, and some workers were unquestionably taken advantage of.

Frederick is commonly categorized as an enemy of workers. Rarely are his principles considered with an open mind and in the context of the era when they were created. In Frederick's system, if a worker was hired, trained, and helped by management but was unable to produce the expected amount for a fair day's work, they were either let go from the job or repositioned in a new job that better fit them. Many leaders and organizations today don't practice this seemingly obvious personnel responsibility. Any company that doesn't practice this is doing the individual a great disservice by keeping them in a job they are not fit for and cannot find success in—especially if the employer has taken the time to train and develop them. How can an individual find prosperity if held to expectations they cannot meet? How can a fish be expected to thrive on land when it is able to breathe only underwater? Frederick's mentality and approach to labor is far from evil. It takes courage to be honest and have challenging conversations. It takes a coward to simply shrug and pretend nothing is happening, which then causes layoffs because the company was not willing to change, to evolve.

The principles of scientific management evolved structured work and provided it with valuable boundaries so strangers could work together and find success. This was no easy riddle to solve, and the solution is something brilliant that we far too commonly overlook and rarely appreciate.

Frederick's nature was the vital element that fueled the creation of the principles of scientific management. Clearly, with an undertaking of this magnitude—introducing new work design principles to a hostile collective—mistakes and errors are all but inevitable. If we judge and critique his principles harshly and with a modern eye, we easily overlook the heroic accomplishment and its positive impact. Once we learn more about Frederick, we begin to unravel the drive behind the principles, and we can see their role in elevating prosperity for the collective. While the principles, in some ways, seem strict to the modern reader, we must remember they were designed to provide clarity in a structured work design during a time of confusion and chaos.

Originally, my opinion of Frederick Winslow Taylor and the principles of scientific management was not a pretty one. Judging by popular literature—even considering books that didn't criticize him but simply wrote about the principles of scientific management from a historical perspective —it seemed that his philosophy was responsible for sucking the meaning out of professional work. The dissatisfaction many today feel with their professional work, the loss of purpose and fulfillment in professional work, and the mundane nature of professional work seem to have been caused by Frederick's principles. The ideas inherent in scientific management seemed cold blooded in the way that they removed the individuality of workers from their profession. Frederick appeared a murderer of the craftsman's art with his belief that generations of craftsman's knowledge could be completely replaced with one ultimate system. Simply put, the principles of scientific management appeared responsible for deskilling our workforce and making workers easily replaceable.

Naturally, deskilling was one outcome of the simplification of work. Each worker focused only on a small, simple task. Critics say Frederick used people like cogs in a machine, caring only about the efficiency of the machine and not about its parts: profit above all else, and an obsessive focus on upholding the process standards.

While critics of Frederick and the principles of scientific management may have good intentions, and while their arguments are warranted, such criticisms are overwhelmingly one sided.

The principles of scientific management provided an answer for the Industrial Revolution's labor challenge. Without one, society would have remained in chaos. Without the organization and management of people, it would be impossible to profitably run a factory. A thoughtful personnel strategy is essential as work design increases in complexity.

Frederick's principles are valuable and should be thoughtfully considered as companies and individuals adapt and calibrate to the modern era of professional work. Modern times will still require job design, but we can modify and design work opportunities. Individuals and companies will need to participate in selection at a higher frequency, as the average person will work with twelve to fifteen different companies over the course of their career (in other words, participate in selection and training).

Additionally, cooperation is as necessary as ever: individuals and companies must work together cordially, many times as strangers. Finally, the complexity and dynamism of professional work today will require the expertise and talents of a gamut of individuals, encouraging the creation of diverse teams (division of labor). Without transparency and fair exchange, individuals and companies will cease to produce their best professional work. The companies that modernize the principles of scientific management will design work in ways that individuals can come together and create something that one individual could only dream of.

How each one of the principles is utilized and the work is designed will depend on the context of the profession and situation. A general overarching personnel system doesn't seem realistic: as famously discovered by United States Air Force analyst Lt. Gilbert Daniels in his study of cockpits, there is no such thing as an average pilot. Therefore, if you design a cockpit to fit the average pilot, you've actually designed it to fit no one. What we can take away from this finding is if you design something for everyone, you design something for no one. Instead, the modern era requires everyone to accept a new level of responsibility in curating their own professional portfolios—something I will discuss later in this book—and for companies to design a diverse catalog of attractive work opportunities for individuals in all seasons of life.

In a way, we are all gardening in a unique environment, trying to figure out what exactly our soil (or soul) is best suited for. What work are we called to do? What kind of professional work do we find interest in? What profession will provide us with purpose, meaning, and fulfillment? What are the talents we must cultivate so we can share our gifts with the world? A quest, an adventure, a journey that only we, as individuals, can embark on in order to discover the answers to such questions. Our professional work can again be a part of who we are, something that we are connected to, interested in, and derive meaning from. However, it will take effort, suffering, and sacrifice on our part. It will demand a change in perspective and taking the path less traveled. We must enter the forest in the place we deem darkest, for our talents are far from obvious when we look forward but are as clear as day looking backward. In a way, the first step must be out of the mist.

In the words of Frederick Winslow Taylor, "We can see and feel the waste of material things. Awkward, inefficient, or ill-directed movements of men, however, leave nothing visible or tangible behind them. Their appreciation calls for an act of memory, an effort of the imagination. And for this reason, even though our daily loss from this source is greater than our waste of material things, the one has stirred us deeply, while the other has moved us but little." Where Frederick saw the waste from the inefficiencies in work design, I see loss in the undiscovered talents that lie dormant within us all. I once overheard a conversation in which a retired woman said something that stuck in my mind: "I have lived my life." However, what I heard was "I am ready to die"—she was saying that every day she woke up with no purpose, no meaning, no excitement or adventure, avoiding anything new or out of the ordinary, becoming an idle creature simply waiting to pass, one of those depicted in a symbolic picture of a line of individuals holding their two coins, waiting for Charon to return from ferrying away the other souls.

How many living dead do we have among us who inhabit the wasteland, still full of life and gifts to share but lacking the clarity or courage to do so? What is life if you are simply idle? As living creatures, we are meant to work, and as humans we can do that in a variety of different ways. We are creatures of curiosity, curious about not only the outer world but also our inner world and who we are. The best way to test our curiosity is to test life—in other words, to collect experiences. If we begin to adjust our attitude toward professional work, its importance for who we are and who we can become, and appreciate its value to life, maybe inevitably what we are left with is interesting work.

PART 3
INTERESTING WORK

Normality is a paved road, it's comfortable to walk but no flowers grow.

— VINCENT VAN GOGH

9
THE ADVENTURE

Some journeys take us far from home. Some adventures lead us to our destiny.

— C.S LEWIS

Today's modern individual picks a major, graduates, and then works in a profession till retirement so they can then have the freedom to do the things they really want to do. The apprenticeships of the craft era are nonexistent, and the initiation that was sacred to our ancestors has been forgotten. Even though some companies market apprenticeships, they are really internships with the wrong name. Today far too many engage in jobs, not professional work. Modern individuals have fallen sway to the sweet enchantment of the Faustian bargain, most without even knowing it. We can say that we are poor at creating jobs that individuals will find meaningful or fulfilling, but what it really comes down to is that we are poor at selecting individuals for professional work and poor at identifying what professional work we feel called to do (or we lack courage to pursue the professional work that interests us). The former reflects the design of structured work and is the consequence of Frederick's principles. The latter is a fracture in our relationship to professional work and results from recognizing neither its importance nor the opportunity and optionality of the modern world. In this era, many individuals have the optionality to participate in work they find interesting, meaningful, connected to, and fulfilling, a.k.a. interesting professional work. However, to engage in such work we must accept the call to adventure in discovering and developing our talents. As Voltaire said, we must cultivate our gardens.

In modern times, the words *profession*, *career*, and *work* are commonly interchangeable. They all have come to represent the same thing—what an individual does for a living; that is, to earn money—but I believe they shouldn't. Instead, we should rethink what "work" is and what it means to us as humans. Words are important, and the meaning we, as a collective, give them influences our relationship with what they signify.

One neglected, forgotten, and misused word can help us make the shift of attitude toward our professional work. That word is *vocation*. The etymology of vocation is as follows: *voco* is a noun that can be translated as "voice," or, in Italian, "expression of opinion." *Vocare* is Latin for "to call," "to name," or "to invoke." *Vocation*, therefore, signifies an inclination to undertake a certain kind of work, especially a religious career, often in response to a perceived summons, a calling—an occupation for which a person is suited, trained, or qualified.

Originally, the term *vocation* was used to describe the journey of an individual into priesthood. To become a priest, you need to feel—and believe—that you had been called to the church directly by God. The idea of being called to one's work is far from novel and dates to the earliest civilizations and societies, in which medicine men, oracles, and mystic ones could hear voices no one else could. They could communicate with the gods, heal the sick, and see into the future. They were called to their work.

There once was a time when the professional work we did was deeply connected to who we were as individuals. It was a part of us, embedded in our personality, persona, and character. As we aged and became no longer fit to work in the same capacity, our professional work changed to match our season of life. In early civilizations, the elderly would be responsible for teaching the children, while the parents engaged in the work their parents once did. The origin of division of labor can be seen here, as a natural example of the gestalt idea that a sum is more than its individual parts.

The modern era is changing the design of professional work, in many ways for the better. Remote work provides individuals the opportunity to live where they please, enabling families to see each other more. Flexible schedules empower individuals to balance their lives accordingly. It is special to be at a point when collectively we can pursue vocational—in other words, interesting—work: that is, work we feel drawn or connected to, or which we find meaningful.

"If you find a job you love, you never work a day in your life" is not what I mean when I talk about interesting work. Loving your work is wonderful and a clear signal of a possible vocation, but it's the meaning behind the work that brings a sacred nature to it. This creates a connection to and respect for the professional work you engage in. Think of the way a master chef respects the kitchen, the artistic process of presenting the food, the experience for the patrons and team members. When you respect the craft, the work, you find the sacred qualities of it that seem to transcend all things. Part of developing a sacred relationship with work is accepting the call to adventure, embarking on the hero's journey.

The shape that our vocational work takes changes and evolves over time, although its essence remains the same, just as an artist may paint one year, another year act, and another year sing. Or a doctor may one year do surgery, another year work as a CEO of a startup, and another year become an author. Your vocation is what you are called to do; it is an expression of who you are and offers a glimpse of what you can become. Developing a curiosity about your vocation and then a connection with your work creates the opportunity for you to experience life authentically. The individual who identifies and engages in interesting professional work experiences a journey full of challenges and treasures designed for them, while the individual who doesn't search for their vocation rarely finds it and therefore faces challenges they don't deem worthy or interesting and discovers empty treasure chests.

Unfortunately, we are not born with a tag that outlines our talents or what our vocational work is. Instead, we must accept the call to adventure and develop the courage to take a leap of faith into the depths of the unknown. For each generation needs heroes, and anyone who embarks on the adventure of finding their vocational work and mastering it is heroic. It's a journey that must be pursued alone, although help along the way is essential. There is a hero inside everyone waiting to be unleashed. There are dormant embers of talent in everyone, eagerly waiting to be ignited.

As humans we have a great gift and a curse: acute consciousness and remarkable abilities. We are too intelligent to sit around idle, and we have the ability to create amazing works. In a way we all behave like miniature gods, creating things daily. Our work is a part of who we are, whether we are professional athletes or university professors. To engage in interesting work, regardless of our profession, we must take the same journey, one that embodies the development of the hero. In other words, the development of the individual.

One way to understand who we are is to experience life —live our life—and if we can spend our time engaging in professional work that we are connected to and find meaningful, we can reach depths and heights that are borderline impossible otherwise. An MMA fighter, Israel Adesanya, once in a fight mouthed "I am prepared to die" to his opponent. Needless to say, he won the fight. Fighting is Adesanya's calling. He loves the profession of fighting and everything that comes with it: the different styles, the training, the culture, and the adventure of self-discovery. He is willing to go all in, just as Spartan warriors did in their time.

Warriors have been present in every era; the difference is that some choose to be warriors and others are forced to be soldiers. Adesanya is not just an MMA fighter but a warrior. There is a difference. There are a few fighters in the MMA—or any professional sport—who are there due to genes and talent, not because it's their calling. They may find some success, but their stay will be short lived. There will come a point at which they will reach a ceiling and come across a true warrior like Adesanya—he will make them question their decision to fight. Don't let your talent take you somewhere your character cannot keep you.

Finding interesting work is the reward; everything that comes with it is a bonus. With money, you can care for your family, hire better people, use better products, and eliminate tasks and problems. Financial benefits help make your profession easier to engage with by eliminating unnecessary distractions, such as working a so-called job—in other words, something you are motivated to do only for money; if you didn't need money, you would never consider doing it.

As we've discussed, previous generations did not have the luxury of professional work options that the collective has today. Now, technological advancements have provided access to information, education, and experts on any profession or topic we could be interested in. However, with optionality comes paralysis of choice. Being overwhelmed with options leads to overchoice and many times prevents us from making any choice at all.

Unfortunately, some of us, consciously or unconsciously, outsource key decisions in our lives to others, following the lead of whatever figures we happen to see around us. That strategy is not one suited for a hero or for the discovery of interesting work. To become a hero, an individual must enter the forest at the place they deem the darkest. A hero must complete their own adventures, the ones that are awaiting them and only them. Only Perseus could defeat Medusa, only Prometheus could steal fire from the gods, and only Perceval could find the Holy Grail.

Regret is the echo of adventures not taken and the howls of monsters not slain. Heroes make mistakes, but rarely do they have regrets, for accepting the call to adventure may not end as expected, but it does reveal and reward.

All heroes are collectors of the secrets of the cosmos, the types of secret that can only be understood with experience and initiation—the latter part being the trials of adventure.

The fortunate few who find their vocation are always deemed unique or privileged. While there is some truth to that, maybe they just had the courage to say yes to the adventure, to answer their inner voice that was calling to them. At the end of the day, the professional work we engage in is meant to be an adventure. Finding interesting work, or identifying what one is called to, helps an individual navigate their quest to becoming a hero—or, in other words, becoming who they are. Seeking our interest, learning who we are, and cultivating a profession around it is a quest and adventure that we must accept responsibility for and pursue individually: a true hero's journey.

10

THE JOURNEY

Faithless is he that says farewell when the road darkens.

— JR. TOLKIEN

J oseph Campbell is responsible for the popularity of the concept of the hero's journey. His portfolio of work and the iconic book *The Hero of a Thousand Faces* introduced the idea of the hero's journey to many. It is an understatement to say that Campbell's theories heavily influenced *Path Paver*. It was his ideas, coupled with those of Ralph Waldo Emerson and Carl Jung, that helped me outline the idea of path paving. Their ideas are the ones we must draw on to rebuild our relationship to professional work, and the framework of the hero's journey is our compass.

Since the first orators brought stories to life around a fire, the outline of every tale has been that of a hero's journey. In its simplest form, becoming a hero requires the completion of three phases: separation, initiation, and return. First, the individual must accept the call to adventure and separate from the status quo of their world. The world needs saving, yet the "becoming" hero doesn't know how to do it and is not connected to their own powers, which offer the saving elixir. The hero discovers and develops a connection with their talents and powers during the journey. This is the initiation phase. Trials prepare the hero for the dragon fight that is to come. In the final test of initiation, the individual must be willing to sacrifice themself to save the world, and by doing so they fulfill their destiny, shedding the skin of the former self to become the elevated hero. Once the hero rises victorious in the final dragon fight, or test, they return to the world and bestow on it the elixir of life, elevating the status quo for everyone.

PHASE 1: CALL TO ADVENTURE

You must be willing to leave the life that you planned in order to find the one waiting for you.

—Joseph Campbell

The first phase is to accept the call to adventure, and this can be understood as the call to life, the call to live. There comes a time in everyone's life when they begin listening to the voice inside or they begin ignoring it. The voice inside is the one urging the acceptance of the call to adventure, to begin living—experiencing life—of one's own accord. The serendipitous nature of life will continuously create opportunities for us to hear the voice, but it takes open eyes to see it. Some people walk through life struggling to recognize luck and opportunities even though they're surrounded by them. Their blindness reflects that they're walking someone else's path instead of paving their own.

The adventure that we are ready for is the one that calls to us. We may not believe we are prepared, but that is part of the journey. The first step is accepting the call to adventure, whether that be in a serendipitous manner or by purposely entering the cave we fear most. It is vital that we accept our call by listening to the voice inside and not the noise outside. The destination is unknown, but the direction can be clear if we take the time to look inward.

Often, individuals who engage in interesting work mention an unexplainable pull, draw, or push toward something. It is hard for them to answer the question, How did you know that was what you wanted to do? This makes sense because when they accepted the call, they didn't know what was to come. In other words, they were coddiwompling—English slang for traveling in a purposeful manner toward a vague destination.

PHASE 2: INITIATION

The struggles you face introduce you to your strengths.

—Epictetus

The second step, initiation, is about discovering, developing, and unleashing the persona of the hero inside us. It's like the famous quote that Michelangelo never said, "I saw an angel trapped in the rock, and I just carved stone away to let her free." Or how Nietzsche, in *Thus Spake Zarathustra*, talks about the necessity of passing through three stages of metamorphosis—Camel, Lion, and Child—before achieving freedom. The idea is sprinkled everywhere throughout history: an initiation is an essential phase on the journey to becoming a hero. We must earn the title of hero; we cannot buy it.

The attitude we have toward the initiation process heavily influences what kind of hero we become. Heroes and villains are different in myths, but in our life's narrative, they are one and the same. We are the hero and villain of our story, the Jekyll and the Hyde. Everyone has a shadow to their light. If we have the courage to unleash the monster of the shadow in order to integrate it, then we can combine the light and the dark to become whole, or complete. In the shadows our dormant talents lie; if we venture into the shadows willingly, we can find the answers we seek. If we move in the shadows by force, we will focus on getting out and miss the answers that lie right in front of us. The answers are always there in the shadows—it's our ability to see them that determines whether we discover them or not. The power of attitude and perspective should not be overlooked.

The crucial part of the initiation phase is releasing the former self to make room for the new self. Part of initiation is growth and expansion, which naturally needs space. It is like a growing child wearing a shirt that is too small. The fear of letting go and the act of holding on to our current selves interferes with the development of the hero. Just as a snake sheds its skin and the moon sheds it shadow, we must shed our former self to become a hero. By no means is this easy, and sacrificing the former self is among one of the most challenging aspects of the journey. The moment of self-sacrifice proves the individual's courage and development. This is where we become a hero, in this transformation. The dragons are slain, the elixir is distributed to the people, and the newly crowned hero elevates the status quo for the collective around them.

When we pursue interesting work and begin path paving, we discover things not found on the well-paved path. These initiations test us but also teach us. Through these challenges, experiences, and moments, we cultivate our individuality and find clarity in who we are, what we can become, and what we are capable of. Without these initiations, we fail to earn the courage necessary to try new things, and we fail to develop the self-reliance to path-pave.

Take the example of Tinker Hatfield, a prominent Nike shoe designer, who discovered by accident that he could draw. After an injury that ended his former career, he enrolled in an architecture class and came to discover he was a gifted artist. If Hatfield never learned he could draw, the opportunity to design shoes for Nike would never have blossomed, and then we would never have the portfolio of iconic shoes Hatfield produced at Nike, such as the Nike Air Max.

PHASE 3: RETURN

> *When the hero quest has been accomplished... the adventurer still must return with his life transmuting trophy. The hero shall now begin the labor of bringing the runes of wisdom, the Golden Fleece, or his sleeping princess back into the kingdom*

of humanity, where the boon may redound to the renewing of the community, the nation, the planet, or the ten thousand worlds.

—Joseph Campbell

The hero now returns to the world from their quest, shares their newly gained gifts, and awaits the call for the next adventure. The return is necessary and just as vital as the separation, for the newly acquired gifts can enhance the world in a positive manner. Just as Alice must return from Wonderland, the hero must return home to share their gifts.

After we discover our interesting work, it's our responsibility to share it with the world. What good is it to find interesting work if we don't participate in it and become a professional? Bob Ross did over four hundred episodes of *The Joy of Painting* and earned very little for it—not because he was not worth it but because there was not much money in public television at the time. This did not stop him from filming them, though, because he recognized that by creating *The Joy of Painting*, he was sharing his gift, he was participating in interesting professional work, and he was making a positive impact doing it. This is the case with all individuals who engage in interesting professional work: what they produce makes a positive impact for others. It is one thing to discover our interests, it's another thing to cultivate them, and it's another thing to become professional. The return is about turning your interest into professional work.

11

PURSUIT OF VOCATION

All men can be criminals, if tempted. All men can be heroes if inspired.

— G.K. CHESTERTON

The separation, initiation, and return journey is required for an individual who wishes to find and pursue interesting work. It is doubtful that modern individuals will imitate the career paths of the generation before, in which the average person worked at one company for most of their professional career and performed more or less the same job—even with promotions. We most likely will work at a variety of different companies, will change work professions, and will reinvent ourselves far more frequently. To the modern individual, the work journey is identical to the hero's journey.

For us, answering the call to adventure means stepping off the well-paved path and beginning to path-pave in search of interesting work. In this phase, we must listen to the voice inside that pushes us to discover what work is of interest to us. Although the answer may seem obvious when we look back, it never is in the beginning. Initiation comes after we've found the professional work we feel called to, interested in, excited about, or inspired to do. In this phase we learn to understand our work, making room for the individual to become and shedding the former self. This is not to be confused with starting over. A twenty-foot snake doesn't shed its skin and become a ten-foot snake; nor does a moon become smaller when it sheds its shadow. Each time a snake sheds its skin, it can expand, and each time a moon sheds its shadow, it shines brighter.

Initiation, or mastering the work, is development and becoming, with the goal of finding our authentic self in the professional work we do. We see this clearly in athletes who reach world-class levels: the way they play their sport is authentically a reflection of who they are. Take Stephen Curry: he plays basketball in a way that is unquestionably Curry-esque. Then there's the boxer Vasiliy Lomachenko, whose style of boxing is unlike anything the sport has ever seen. This is what we are after: finding work that we are called to and merging our personality and who we are with that work to create something unique and different. The individual who does this is a hero to the world. They expand and grow the profession in a way that would be impossible by any other means.

Returning is coming back from our adventure and cultivating the interesting work to create something we can do professionally. We must share our gifts and engage in our interesting work in a manner that goes beyond the recreational. In this manner, we will continue to cultivate our bond and relationship to that work. This is no different from the way we cultivate bonds or relationships with loved ones. It takes time, patience, energy, resilience, and commitment.

While sometimes I think it would be nice if we all were born with tags naming our vocational work or purpose, clearly that is not the case, and I have come to love that. While today most of the world does not engage in interesting work, those who do have one thing in common: they paved their own path. Every one of them accepted the call to adventure, slew dragons, entered caves they feared, and made it out to the other side of the adventure reborn, stronger and more capable than before, having unleashed the dormant powers within.

It's the call to adventure that gets our attention and ignites the courage within us to accept it. We must leave the paved path, depart from what is expected of us by society and the world around us, and learn what it is we expect of ourselves, separating ourselves from the noise of the world to find the signal within. It's the progress that feels good in this phase: to keep moving, keep searching, keep being courageous.

When we see world-class individuals engaging in their professional work in an authentic way, it's beautiful, almost enchanting in a way. Deep inside, even if we are not familiar with the hero's journey or with these individuals' backgrounds, we know they had to endure suffering to cultivate such a gift. Conversely, the world is littered with individuals who are thought to have wasted their talents, but maybe they just missed the opportunity to apply their talents in the right profession. Talents are wasted only if they are never discovered and developed. An individual who doesn't make it to professional level in their sport does not have to start over or "waste" their talents and do something else. Instead, this individual needs to accept the call to adventure and begin figuring out what other talents they have and what other types of work they find interest in.

In terms of interesting work, a compelling aspect of the hero's journey is that it anticipates that individuals will make their way through the adventure a few times in life, especially in the modern world. Additionally, it removes culturally pervasive time and age limitations. Early societies utilized elderly people far more intelligently than we do today. Elders played roles within their communities as teachers and counselors. Today we rarely take advantage of the wisdom and experience of older individuals, partly because of the modern career mindset of the race to retirement and partly because as individuals age, they stop developing their talents, and companies are rarely creative enough to find a useful role for them.

With the framework of the hero's journey as a guide, individuals can take control of discovering and developing their talents regardless of age or season of life. As we all know by now, age is not the best predictor of skills, abilities, or talents for many lines of professional work. The traditional goal of a job was to earn enough to retire and either do nothing or do the thing you always wanted to do. The former will kill you slowly: *Homo sapiens* is not meant for idleness; some sort of work, purpose, or meaning is necessary to live. For some that may come in the form of being a grandparent and watching little ones; for others, it might be taking up a new hobby, like gardening or painting. Either way, dedicating energy toward something of meaning, and something that is challenging and that we can focus on mastering, is a necessity.

Experience is the hallmark of the hero's journey toward interesting work. Some things in life simply cannot be understood with words alone; experience is the only teacher. For example, hunters of one Aboriginal tribe explain that the most important forms of knowledge can't be taught in words. Knowledge of this kind, they insist, can't be taught because it resides not just in their minds but also in their bodies, and because it finds expression in skills that could never be reduced to mere words.

In the same way, heroes are made, not born. While an individual may be born with heroic talents and abilities, if they do not develop them and face the monsters they fear, they will never become a hero. Everyone alive has a hero inside of them; only a few develop the courage to become it.

Understanding your season of life and leveraging the hero's journey as a guide to interesting work can release the pressure of choosing a job and the suffocating hold the Faustian bargain has on most of us. To live is to work, and to live a life worth living is to live authentically by discovering who you are. The only way a hero becomes a hero is through their own adventure. If you are alive, you have a hero inside of you, regardless of age, demographic, ethnicity, or anything else.

When we define work as the transfer of energy, we can be thoughtful and considerate of how we utilize our energy on a daily, monthly, and yearly basis. It's a freeing mindset, one that releases the chains the Faustian bargain so slyly wraps around us. Many of us are voluntary prisoners—not prisoners to companies or employers but prisoners to ourselves. We don't offer ourselves permission to do the work we are interested in, or even to discover what it could be. Life is meant to be an interesting adventure, an experience, and the only way for it to be that is to pave your own path.

PART 4
VOCATIONAL MINDSET

The job at which one works is not what counts, but rather the manner in which one does the work. It does not lie with the occupation, but always with us, whether those elements of the personal and the specific which constitute the uniqueness of our existence are expressed in the work and thus make life meaningful.

[...]

Only when he goes beyond the limits of purely professional service, beyond the tricks of the trade, does he begin that truly personal work which alone is fulfilling.

— VIKTOR FRANKL

12

A PERSPECTIVE SHIFT

It is what is commonly called Vocation... [which] acts like a law of God from which there is no escape... Anyone with a vocation hears the inner voice; they are called.

— CARL JUNG

As we continue to transition into a new era, an evolution in our approach to professional work is necessary, just as it was over one hundred years ago during the Industrial Revolution. Today, individuals and companies are overwhelmed by the depth and breadth of work optionality. However, now more than any other time in history, a vast majority of individuals have the opportunity to engage in interesting work and to participate in a profession they are connected to. What seems to be holding us back is the need to change the way we think about work. Part of the journey of the modern era will be to evolve our attitudes and perspectives about work.

Individuals and companies are now responsible for developing innovative ideas about what future professions and careers could be. Organizations must develop opportunities that are interesting, and individuals must understand what kind of work they are interested in. The change requires individuals to develop their professional portfolios and offer the world talents, skills, and abilities that are needed and valuable. Individuals and companies must collaborate in this effort, as it is not yet clear what this new work design should look like.

Roles are changing and being invented too quickly for companies to truly map out career paths. Individuals have access to information like never before, which makes changing professional paths possible. Personnel processes will need to be structured in a way to easily calibrate for different types of relationships. Where the relationship used to be between company and employee, it will become between company and individual, and this leads to an increase in the importance of reputational currency.

The writing on the wall seems clear: a new approach to work is necessary, hence the reintroduction of the original definition of vocational work and the work design of interesting professional work. We must design professional work with a flexible and antifragile attitude. Interesting work design acknowledges that to work is to live. Everything that is living is working. We must adopt a more encompassing definition and understanding of work. Instead of professional work being a necessary evil, full of forced sacrifices and Faustian bargains, it can regain its sacred nature and become a part of who we are.

Crucially, if the professional work we engage in is not something we are interested in and find meaning in, it will take a toll on us. Maybe in the form of burnout or anxiety;

maybe something else. One way or another, we pay a price. Following the well-paved path and turning our backs on the responsibilities of paving our own will foster a stew of regret, a ruthless form of suffering. The "lucky" or "good" professional work situation is a manipulative trap that we all can fall prey to.

Fortunately, by altering our perspective and attitude about work, we begin to develop immunities to such trickery. The interesting work design is not for everyone, nor is it necessarily always the best way to approach professional work; it is simply another option. There will always be some individuals who are interested in the structured and safe work design, and these individuals can be wonderful people.

However, the structured and safe work design can be a slippery slope if we are not careful. One promotion leads to another, and the job becomes a career we were not pursuing and, worst of all, are not interested in. The money and benefits become a part of our lifestyle and who we are, and then we are prisoner to the job and the money. We're like the frog who sits in a pot of water that slowly heats up, unaware as it comes to a boil. This is how a person becomes a "successful" individual who is wealthy but miserable. In this position, we can afford to purchase any material desire but lack meaningful relationships—family, friends, work. We can go anywhere in the world but have no one to go with.

Let's be clear: money is important, but when it's the main factor in our professional decisions, we lose sight of other, equally important elements. We struggle with professional work decisions when the compensation is stacked in front of us. Rarely do we acknowledge the importance of choice when we consider our profession. As my father once told me, if you walk with a man with a limp, over time you will develop a limp. This is partly why it's so valuable to begin to understand who we are and to develop a connection and relationship with our vocation. If we engage in work we do not like, are not fit for, and have no connection with or interest in, sure enough, over time, a limp will develop.

I believe that we all are called to do some kind of professional work. The challenge comes in figuring out what that work is, transitioning through the different seasons of the work journey, and enduring it. Carl Jung had a theory that individuals should focus not on perfection but on becoming (also known as the process of individuation). We should seek to learn and get to know our authentic self—to have the humility and honesty with ourselves to acknowledge that elements of our individuality lie dormant. Only a brave individual will journey to the depths of their soul to discover who they are.

Individuals who engage in interesting work move differently in the world; they are lighter. Those who are trapped by the Faustian bargain walk heavily and feel the weight of the prison chains as each year passes.

But what is your calling, and how do you discover it? This is a challenging question to answer, if not all but impossible for some. Our calling is rarely obvious—until we find it. Who we are and our vocation are like one of those heart necklaces that you break into two so you can give one half to your mate. Or they're a message in a bottle that is roaming the ocean, and you are on a quest to find it because it has the answers to your deepest desires. It has the map of the world's greatest treasures.

Path Paver was written to act as a guide for individuals to approach work from the perspective of a vocation instead of a job. Interesting work design looks to free the job-mindset individual from the fallacies and hollow barriers that trap them in professional work they feel stuck in. If at least a few accept the call to adventure, how will our relationship with professional work change over the coming generations? Professional work can be positive for the collective—or, at the very least, no longer a necessary evil, a prison sentence, but instead interesting, meaningful, worthwhile. Or as Carl Jung would say, a pursuit toward individuation.

In the final chapter, we'll explore interesting work design, leveraging the idea of path paving: what it is, how to become a path paver, and what to expect.

13
PATH PAVER

They were always making discoveries by accidents and sagacity, of things they were not in quest of...now do you understand serendipity?

— HORACE WALPOLE

Developing the agency to pave your own path, to become a path paver, changes the manner in which you interact with your world. Instead of things getting in your way, things are simply part of the way. The former reflects the perspective of the path follower, in which barriers that block off the paved path are an annoyance, an inconvenience. The latter reflects the perspective of the path paver, in which a barrier is simply there, and you can choose to go over it, around it, under it, or through it—or even avoid it.

If we trace the paths of successful individuals, each will be different and idiosyncratic, but they will have at least one thing in common: their shapes will not be straight or even squiggly lines. They'll be labyrinths that twist and turn inside. The objective is not for a career path to form an image of a line ascending from left to right—the standard symbol for growth. When it comes to path paving, the standard signal for growth is one that turns inward.

So let's create some simple definitions to outline the idea of path paving.

WHAT IS A PATH PAVER?

A foolish consistency is the hobgoblin of little minds, adored by little statesmen and philosophers and divines. With consistency a great soul has simply nothing to do.

—Ralph Waldo Emerson

A path paver is an individual who pursues and participates in interesting professional work of their own accord. A path paver sometimes follows well-paved paths but is not restricted or bound to them. They pick and choose when they follow and when they pave. This optionality creates new experiences and enables individuality. Their individuality enables them to participate in their professional work in a way that is authentic and unique.

A path follower is an individual who pursues and participates in a profession following the outlined career path. A path follower will deviate from the paved path only if they are forced to or if they believe they have something to gain. Otherwise, the paved path is the way. With each season that goes by, a path follower becomes more and more dependent on the paved path, or in other words, they weaken their agency to pave their own way. Their lack of optionality limits their opportunities for unique experiences, suffocating their individuality, and they participate in their professional work in a way that is general and standard.

HOW DO I PATH-PAVE?

To be great is to be misunderstood.

—Ralph Waldo Emerson

You can path-pave any way you desire. There isn't a way to path-pave; there is only a way not to path-pave, which is remaining chained to the paved path, following already outlined career paths.

To begin path-paving in pursuit of interesting work, follow an interest. Accept the call to adventure. Be open to how it may show up. It could be an invitation to something you normally would not go to, an ask you normally would not receive, a request to help in a way you are interested in but have never gotten the opportunity for. As a path paver you are wandering but are not lost. When you don't worry about following the paved path, you can direct your attention to the opportunities around you.

PATH-PAVING PHASES

As you proceed through life, following your own path, birds will shit on you. Don't bother to brush it off. Getting a comedic view of your situation gives you spiritual distance. Having a sense of humor saves you.

—Joseph Campbell

We path-pave in pursuit of three different professional work purposes: searching, mastering, and sharing. Each purpose is the question with which we begin the call to adventure. It's the question that begins the quest, that sets the adventure on its way. Regardless of the phase, we must complete the hero's journey to find the treasure we seek, the answer to the question we began with. As you can see, having the courage to ask the question is a pivotal point. So, when it comes to interesting professional work, we are path paving to find out what the profession is, to master the profession, or to share our work.

In the searching phase, you are identifying what your interesting professional work is. It's key to follow your interests and try new and different things. Your interests are the clues the adventure gives you, the hero, on your journey. Sometimes a clue comes in the form of an old man or woman who shares a piece of wisdom; sometimes it's in the form of a unique situation that you can choose to avoid or lean in to. Much of path paving is tuning your signal to allow for serendipitous moments and luck to happen to you. Too often we create defenses against them unconsciously because we are so focused on following the paved path. It is as if a man dying of thirst walked past a well because he was blindly following a paved path that was said to lead to water.

In the mastering phase, you are in pursuit of developing a relationship with your profession and expressing yourself in it. You're seeking to do it in a way that is uniquely yours, that reflects your character and personality—your style. Here you begin to try things unconventionally; you test the principles to figure out which are true and which are optional. Here you experiment courageously and relentlessly, integrate your inspiration and profession, and develop the discipline necessary to achieve mastery.

In the sharing phase, you seek to use your gifts, your professional work, to better the lives of others. You're figuring out in what ways your work is valuable, and who it's suited for and can best serve. Based on your style, a preferred group will emerge. Something for everyone is something for no one. Your style naturally creates preferences, which is important for the development of space for other professionals. If you are the only one in a category of work, you cannot be professional; you need to compete against other professionals to be professional. In that way, the competition is the catalyst for the development of the profession. Without it, the profession fails to develop and remains amateur. Path paving provides individuals the room to cultivate their styles, while the paved path restricts individuals to learn the same style.

PATH PAVING

> *In the name of his social image he [Parzival, knight of King Arthur's court] continues the Waste Land principle of acting according to the way you have been told to act instead of the way of the spontaneity of your noble nature (and the adventure fails).*

—Joseph Campbell

The result of becoming a path paver is simple: you have the agency to move in the world as an individual who participates in society in a way that betters the collective and provides you with meaning, purpose, and fulfillment. Participating in interesting professional work is a journey about not linear success but inward success: we discover who we are and what we are capable of, and we experience life differently. Being a path paver means being someone who is ready for their call; a path follower is someone who ignores the call and inhabits the wasteland. The path paver experiences a lifetime of adventure. The path follower forever awaits the adventure of a lifetime. Our professional work is important and can be something we don't wish to end as quickly as possible—something we are interested in and appreciate as a part of who we are.

Our professional work will not be the same every season of life, and it doesn't need to be. Following a paved career path in one profession for thirty-plus years may not make much sense for everyone in the modern era. If our relationship to our professional work changes and the goal of work changes, then we can release ourselves from retirement as the end point of work. Path pavers don't seek retirement but instead seek leisure and freedom to engage in interesting work however they want with no financial restrictions or limitations.

ACCEPT THE CALL TO ADVENTURE: BECOME A PATH PAVER

The achievement of the hero is one that he is ready for, it is a manifestation of his character. And it's amusing the way in which the landscape and the conditions of the environment match the readiness of the hero. The adventure he is ready for is the one he gets... The adventure evokes a quality of his character that he didn't know he possessed.

—Joseph Campbell

In order to identify and engage in interesting work, we must welcome the randomness, the chaos, the unknown, the discomfort, because these are the corners in life in which serendipitous opportunities manifest, where the heroes find the hidden treasures, and where we find answers to the questions we seek. The randomness of the world is essential. Those who pave their own path in pursuit of interesting work will see doors where there were once only walls; doors that were once locked will magically unlock, and the doors you have been knocking on will finally be opened.

An element of accepting the call to adventure is

accepting that any plans we do have are fragile and can change in an instant. When we accept the quest to seek the answer to the question we have, it's better to be prepared than to have a plan that later limits our ability to understand luck. When we plan, we set expectations, and if anything turns out differently, it is considered a challenge or problem to be solved. When we are prepared, we are ready for whatever may unfold. We are open.

Be prepared to be lucky, and in the meantime, focus on paving your own path in your profession. The universe will tilt in your direction soon enough. It's what you do in the shade that dictates what you can do in the light.

AFTERWORD

*Be who you are and say what you feel because those who mind
don't matter and those who matter don't mind.*

— DR. SEUSS

The way we organize and design work evolves as we do.
The rules of the game change, which influences the way we
play it. When professional work design expands from
important work to the opportunity for interesting work, we
see individuals pursuing self-discovery (and self-expres-
sion). When work design shifts from interesting to structured, we find individuals transition into workers, but
doing so in exchange for prosperity, which lifts the next
generation. When we transition from structured to safe
work design, we find employees.

The idea of path paving is far from original. It goes by
many different names; it's been found in the earliest texts
and taught by some of the most interesting minds. The goal
of this book has been to employ the general idea of path
paving to change our perspective to approaching profes-

sional work and to provide an alternative option. While the paved professional path is a viable option, and one well suited to some, it's surely no longer the only viable option and is not suited for everyone.

The chapters above outlined the elements and history of work design and how the modern work design is a hangover of the principles of scientific management (though we often assume it's simply always been this way) and offered a different way to approach professional work. All this has been written with the intention to liberate individuals from feeling pressured to follow restrictive well-paved professional paths.

> *He isn't thinking or living in terms of humanity, he's living in terms of a system. And this is the threat to our lives; we all face it; we all operate in our society in relation to a system. Now is the system going to eat you up and relieve you of your humanity or are you going to be able to use the system to human purposes?*

> —Joseph Campbell

The idea of path paving is not meant to be a universal approach or solution. Instead, it's meant specifically for those who seek an alternative way to participate in professional work. Some individuals prefer structured and safe work design; these people can be excellent professionals and wonderful people, and they're essential to society. Then there are individuals who prefer important and interesting work design. These people, too, can be excellent workers and wonderful people, and they, too, are essential to society.

This is not a conversation about what's better or worse.

It's about trade-offs and making conscious choices. If you choose the structured and safe work design, no problem: at least now you understand the design framework and can navigate it accordingly. If you choose the important and interesting work design, at least now you have an understanding of the responsibility you assume and can navigate it courageously and confidently.

Our season of life or situation in life can influence which work design we accept or are able to choose. Accepting the call to adventure is a luxury that some people do not have. My hope is that that group of people who are unable to accept this call shrinks with each generation, for I love the idea of a world where most people participate in professional work they find interesting.

Ultimately, the principles I apply to professional work are straightforward. I believe the professional work we do is important in discovering who we are and becoming what we can be, and in how we experience life. Chasing retirement is another way of chasing death, for when we cease to have purpose, meaning, or fulfillment in our life, our soul begins to rot. After we finish our career in a profession, we should look to pivot and begin a career in a different profession or engage in our profession differently (really, the options are infinite). This doesn't mean we operate in the same manner; we can be professional in a different way, whether that involves gardening, painting, grandparenting, or anything else under the sun. Ideally, if we retire from one profession, our financial responsibilities will be such that we can make decisions that are not solely monetarily oriented but have the potential to be financially rewarding.

I close with a true story to help illuminate the idea that when we lack purpose or meaning in our life, we become inhabitants of the wasteland, lifeless wanderers—and yet we can free ourselves if we have a purpose, something to live for. That purpose becomes our fuel source, which, when laid across the embers of life, can reignite the fire in our soul.

A dear friend of mine has had cancer for a few years, and it's clear that his time with us here on earth is coming to an end. I had the honor of keeping him company for one of his chemo treatments, and I was quite surprised. His spirit, personality, and energy were high. He was joking with the nurse, was sharp in conversation with me, and had the energy to have a three-hour intellectually deep conversation. If I didn't know better, I would have had a hard time believing this man had cancer and was dying. He seemed more alive than most of the people I'd interacted with that week.

After the chemo treatment, I asked what was a pretty foolish question, all things considered: "How are you feeling?" His answer made me smile and at the same time inspired me.

He responded, "I am juiced up and excited now that I have this to work on, have a purpose, something to do, to focus on—to work on something I am good at."

See, he'd invited me to join him during his chemo treatment because he had just been hired to help sell a business, and he believed I was a qualified buyer for it. My friend had a long and quite successful career in mergers and acquisitions. He is an artist when it comes to designing business deals, bringing buyers and sellers together, and seeing the value for both sides in ways the novice would never notice. With this professional work opportunity (he was getting paid to do it—not that he needed the money, but pay made it professional and real), he was full of life again, moving with purpose. He has at least one final heroic deed to do before his time is up.

At this moment I saw with my own eyes what I had already truly believed: the importance of purpose in life, of having a profession, of being good at something.

Having professional work that we enjoy and find interest and purpose in is just as important as going to the gym or eating healthy. Professional work that gives us purpose does something to our souls, fills us with willpower, gives us hope and belief. It fuels us in a way very few other things can.

Often, I wonder whether depression, anxiety, and other illnesses can be curbed by finding interesting work. If we have purpose in our life, if we have a profession in which we are fulfilled and which provides us with a sense of individuality and meaning, then maybe we can begin to make better decisions. If we love writing but struggle to do it because we don't have time, maybe we will learn to be more thoughtful with how we spend our time. If we love to cook but can't because we are scared of fire, maybe we will conquer our fear of fire. What if finding our profession is a way for us to have a meaningful reason to conquer our greatest fears and the courage to venture into the unknown?

The hero's journey to interesting professional work is a journey to discovering who we are. The adventure cultivates the hero that lies inside all of us through the trials, suffering, and experience of discovering (and participating in) interesting work. The struggle for existence is the struggle *for* something; it is purposeful, and only in so being can it be meaningful and able to bring meaning into life. It's about the professional work we find only by paving our own path. For interesting work is like the Holy Grail: it finds you; you don't find it. I believe that in life we are meant to work in some fashion, and accepting the call to find interesting professional work, master it, and share it with the world is the adventure of a lifetime. In the words of Joseph Campbell, our life evokes our character.

To find the treasures we seek, we must accept the responsibility of paving our own paths. By doing so we become path pavers, immune to the Faustian bargain and Faustian riddle of our era. The goal of professional work does not need to be shortsighted and focus solely on the transaction of time and currency; it can be something much more. Only this question remains: Which path will you choose?

Two roads diverged in a wood, and I—
  I took the one less traveled by,
  And that has made all the difference.

— *ROBERT FROST*

GETTING STARTED
PROFESSIONAL PORTFOLIOS

The mystery of human existence lies not in just staying alive, but in finding something to live for.

— FYODOR DOSTOYEVSKY

When a great leader is hiring, they search for a few things, but none is more significant than evidence of exceptional ability. Depending on the opportunity, the domain, and what can be known, the evidence for this ability looks different. However, common hiring practices center around criteria that rarely correlate with performance or abilities. For one thing, developing criteria is very challenging, but more important, the wrong criteria will lead us to hire the wrong person or prompt an individual to develop skills and abilities that do not support their talents—in other words, to follow a paved path of professional development. Take the individual who pursues a college degree simply because all "good" jobs require one but never uses their degree in their line of work—or, worse, cannot afford to pursue their interesting work because of the student loans they have acquired. Misguided paved paths showcase themselves in a variety of ways; one thing that is universal is that the essential criteria necessary for a job are rarely obvious.

We have an interesting paradox here: if you pave your own path, you will not be viewed as qualified for the work opportunity based on the criteria that are being applied, but if you follow the paved path, you also will struggle to stand out because you will be camouflaged by a sea of résumés from people who did the exact same thing. As Victor d'Argent said in *An Uncommon Way to Wealth*, "Although working odd jobs will broaden your experience, it will keep you the servant of others, rather than your own master. At the same time, it is true that you must probably spend some time as an employee before you have the foundations for creating an enterprise of your own."

The traditional résumé has gone through so many iterations over time that it has lost its value. Within hiring for professional work, the résumé carries far too much weight for its purpose.

The résumé of the last decade has become an exercise in box checking rather than a real reflection of an individual's talents, skills, or abilities. Today, most pay for their résumés to be created, companies barely pay attention to them, and applicant tracking systems are easily hacked. I must beg to ask, Why are we still using them? Where is their value? Résumés are rarely useful, at least the way they are expected to be, and are quickly losing their significance. What will take the place of the résumé is still up for debate. However, I think transitioning from résumés to professional portfolios is an interesting option.

A professional portfolio is something that an individual

is responsible for developing and cultivating. It can include anything the individual finds representative of their STACK (skills, talents, abilities, character, knowledge). In this way, the portfolio can include finished projects, samples, passion work, hobby work, reviews, and so on—anything the individual believes is helpful for a company or partner to understand the professional work they can do, the work they want to do, and the types of opportunities they are seeking.

The traditional résumé functions as a gatekeeper instead of as a warm introduction. With a professional portfolio, individuals can begin to help the hiring ecosystem see a richer picture than that created by redundant résumés, which all read the same. A professional portfolio brings the individual back into focus. Work opportunities of the future are impossible to predict, and to find the talent for the professional work of the unknown, we must begin to understand individuals as a gestalt. In other words, we must look at the whole person, not just their degree (if they have one) and years of experience (if they have any).

While intelligence can be a performance indicator, a college degree does not necessarily equate to intelligence. As Fyodor Dostoyevsky said, "Being intelligent isn't enough to make a good decision." There are plenty of intelligent people who did not earn a college degree. The same can be said about years of experience. While experience is valuable and can be an indicator of judgment and intuition, it does not always indicate level of ability or depth of talent. There are plenty of individuals who have half the experience of their peers but outperform them.

Experience and education are noteworthy, but the way

we weigh them today, using résumés, is shortsighted. The professional portfolio is a way to broaden our perspective of the individual and aid the hiring ecosystem to be thoughtful in the way work opportunities are created.